SELF-DIRECTED CHANGE for the MID-CAREER MANAGER

SELF-DIRECTED CHANGE *for the* MID-CAREER MANAGER

Robert F. Pearse
B. Purdy Pelzer

amacom

A DIVISION OF AMERICAN MANAGEMENT ASSOCIATIONS

Library of Congress Cataloging in Publication Data

Pearse, Robert F
   Self-directed change for the mid-career manager.

   Includes bibliographical references and index.
   1. Executives. 2. Success. 3. Age and employment. I. Pelzer, B. Purdy, joint author. II. Title.
HF5500.2.P4   658.4'09   75-19420
ISBN 0-8144-5385-6

*To the 25 anonymous practicing managers
who herein share with the reader
their mid-career situations.*

Preface

Mid-life, once the forgotten period between early adulthood and old age, has become in the past few years a matter for examination and review, and a number of books have recently been written on the mid-life phenomenon from a variety of perspectives. Since this book is designed primarily for managers, it will focus on the manager in mid-life (who is presumably also in mid-career) and on his unique role in society.

Mid-career can, and should, be a time of challenge and generative growth, to use a phrase developed by Professor Erik H. Erikson of Harvard University. One's personal growth in the middle years can be enhanced considerably by a sharper perspective of events from his past—that is, by an intensive self-examination of the critical incidents that have gone into shaping his life to date. Equally important for insuring such growth are practical suggestions for planning more satisfying alternatives for the future. It is hoped that this book will provide the manager with both—that it will, in other words, serve as a practical, "real world" tool for growth through self-analysis and self-directed change.

Toward that end, guidelines and 25 brief case histories will be provided to enable the manager to evaluate his past career and present mid-career situation and to plan his most probable high-payout moves in the future. The guidelines will cover the following areas:

☐ The work world of the manager in terms of job, organizational dynamics, interpersonal relationships, and career.

☐ The wider world in which the manager lives: his community, state, nation, and so forth.

☐ The manager's interpersonal world: his family, friends, and social relationships off the job.

☐ A social-history summary of what has happened in his lifetime up to this point—with particular emphasis on the depression of the 1930s, World War II, and the period of extreme managerial mobility from 1950 to 1970.

☐ A review of the developmental psychology models of Professor Daniel Levinson of Yale and of Professor Erikson in terms of their implications for today's mid-career manager.

☐ Suggestions for developing a Managerial Mid-Career Balance Sheet as a basis for career and personal development planning. (Chapter 9 contains a number of Self-Analysis Charts designed to assist the reader in setting up the Mid-Career Balance Sheet. Those Charts provide an opportunity for in-depth self-exploration.)

☐ Suggestions for preparing an Action Plan for self-directed change and planned self-development. (Chapter 10 presents a model for translating the Mid-Career Balance Sheet findings into the Action Plan.)

Though intended primarily for the manager in mid-life, this book can also be useful to the younger manager who has recently begun to climb the pyramidal ladder or to the veteran who has already reached the peak. Either may find it helpful in analyzing his present circumstances from a number of different viewpoints. For younger managers it can be additionally useful in helping to prepare them for making successful mid-career choices and judgments when they do reach the middle years.

Because women have moved into managerial positions in large numbers only within the past few years, the subjects of the vignettes presented herein are male managers. However, the concepts and models presented in this book apply equally to managers of both sexes.

The authors join in expressing their appreciation to Dr. Alfred J. Marrow, whose pioneering efforts in the field of human resource development have brought into existence new forms of cooperation in relations between management and employees and have set an example for all who follow.

Professor Pearse contributed to this book while on sabbatical from the Boston University School of Management. He wishes to thank the university administration and Dean Peter Gabriel, S.M.G., for this time away from the usual academic schedule.

A number of concepts and techniques presented here were developed by Professor Pearse over the past ten years in working with individuals in the management development field. In particular, recognition is due to:

☐ Pat Boglioli, Carl Long, and Jay Meagher of the Mobil Corporation's Management Education staff, for work on career development in the Factors of Management Course.

☐ Robert Steinberg, vice-president, Reliance Group, Inc., for collaboration in the company's professional management training course.

☐ Mike Richards, program director, Center for Management Development, American Management Associations, for presenting the first Middlessence course for managers.

☐ Mr. Richards' fellow faculty members in the AMA's Executive Effectiveness Course, in particular Robert Dvorin, Herbert Hayward, Kenneth Recknagle, and Charles Roth, for joint efforts in course design models that combine self-directed change with conventional sensitivity training for managers.

☐ Richard Leider, First National Bank of Minneapolis, and Professor William Weitzel, University of Minnesota, for work on the university's Mid-Career Renewal Seminars.

☐ Professor Max M. Kostick, Boston State College, for our decade of work on managerial-styles analysis in mid-career management.

Robert F. Pearse
B. Purdy Pelzer

Contents

1/Mid-Career Stresses, Problems, and Opportunities

NOT ONLY does the mid-career manager share in all the physiological and sociological predicaments that people in middle life commonly experience in contemporary society, he also faces a set of circumstances peculiar to his managerial role in today's complex organizations. While every occupation has some measure of stresses and problems, the nature of managerial work carries responsibilities and burdens that make that occupation undeniably unique.

KEY ASPECTS OF MANAGERIAL LIFE

"Management," a current definition states, "is the attainment of organizational objectives *with and through people.*" Attaining objectives in complex organizations with and through many different types of individuals requires a special set of skills and abilities.

The key aspects of managerial work include:

The job itself. The manager often has to be a combination of personal doer, interpersonal leader and motivator, and far-seeing administrator.

The organization. The manager gets his results in a variety of organizational situations. Some organizations—usually the professionally managed ones—are well staffed and well run from the top down. Long-range planning, budgeting, manpower utilization and development, and farsighted marketing techniques are their hallmarks.

Most organizations, unfortunately, are not so well run. Cycles of crisis management, financial boom and bust, pressure to increase sales, then production, then sales again are typical of less effectively run organizations. Most managers spend their careers working in organizations that vary somewhere between the ideal and the impossible.

Interpersonal relationships. The manager's interpersonal relationships require him to vary his own style to adjust to each situation. In a crisis he may have to crack down and be the tyrant. In coaching, counseling, and guiding a sensitive subordinate, he may have to act as the kindly father. With his peers, relationships are often a complex blend of competition and collaboration. To complete an assignment that requires joint efforts, he often must collaborate with a peer with whom he is competing for a promotion.

In dealing with authority and power relationships, the manager has to express his own ideas and opinions and sell them to his superiors—if he can. Yet when final decisions are made, he has to carry them out whether he completely agrees with them or not.

The manager at mid-life is frequently confronted with a generation gap between himself and younger employees. Those born in the relatively affluent 1950s have different life values and priorities. They are not always as motivated to work long hours and to give over-and-above commitment to the organization as are most of the depression generation.

Career planning. Career and personal-development planning are relatively new concepts in organizational life. In the past, managers got a job with an organization and tended to work their way up the promotional ladder as far as their abilities and opportunities would take them.

With the rapidly increasing opportunities for managerial mobility that arose in the 1950s and continued through the early 1970s, managers tended to move about rapidly, both within the organization and from one organization to another. The shortage of trained managers during this period led to unusually rapid advancement for many managers who are now in mid-life.

At present many organizations engaged in sophisticated utilization and development of human resources are involving the individual manager more and more in decisions that affect his career. Whereas it was typical in the 1950s and 1960s for the organization to offer the manager a promotional opportunity simply on a take-it-or-leave-it basis, there is now a greater tendency to give him special training in career- and personal-development planning so that he can participate in these kinds of decisions.

Increasingly, managers are turning down what formerly would have been perceived as advancement plums. They are doing this for a variety of reasons. Some do not want to make a geographical change because they and their families enjoy living in a particular location. Others simply do not feel that the psychological and physiological pressures of added responsibilities are worth the extra status and financial rewards.

PROBLEMS OF THE MID-CAREER MANAGER

The manager usually spends a great deal of his waking time and energy either on the job or in thinking about work problems. Short-run work problems are usually of the crisis variety. For example, a particular order is overdue, and all available energy has to be put into getting it out. Or a difficult sale is hanging fire, and the sales manager and his staff go into a "fire-fighting" campaign in order to put it over.

Longer-run problems usually relate to interpersonal relationships and their effects on the manager's career opportunities and job securities. Cutbacks during periods of recession and decreased profits cause uncertainties and stresses. The arrival of a new boss

—particularly if he is from another organization—often requires a good deal of adjustment on the manager's part. How he stands with the new man, how his performance will be evaluated, whether he will be taken into the new boss's inner circle or left outside all have a direct bearing on his own psychological security.

Reorganizations, which are particularly chronic in the fast-growth organization, create another set of problems for the manager in mid-career. In reorganizations, new responsibilities and power patterns emerge. Some men move up and advance. Others stay at the same level. Still others may be demoted directly or indirectly or may even choose to leave. At best, frequent reorganizations are upsetting to interpersonal and work-group relationships. New communications channels have to be developed. New influence and decision-making networks have to be explored and tested.

STRESSES OF THE MID-CAREER MANAGER

Managerial mid-career stresses result from a number of different causes. Work-related stresses derive from the particular nature of managerial work in complex organizations. In general, such stresses relate to the problems just outlined.

Another set of stresses results from the manager's typical preoccupation with work and career. Because he is often a highly competitive and achievement-oriented individual, the manager tends to build a lopsided life. In pursuit of job challenge and career advancement he often narrows his life and interests to the point where his ego is so totally involved in work that he has difficulty relating to others on a spontaneous, informal, relaxed basis.

Intense work-role specialization is encouraged both by organizations and by a society that values the standard of living that results from successfully managed organizations. The manager who works extremely long hours, who neglects or gives minimal attention to his family, and who has little time or energy left for close friendships or participation in civic affairs is still considered a significant and, indeed, an important member of our society.

AL, THE MANAGER WHO WORKED OVERTIME

Al is a manager who decided to change his compulsive "workaholic" life-style in mid-life so he could enjoy the benefits of a more balanced way of living. As one of a group of 30 men who were in on the beginning of a new business, Al had regularly scheduled himself three or four hours of paperwork each night, Monday through Friday. He usually spent Saturdays at meetings or working in the engineering department, where he was chief engineer.

His wife suggested that he build an office in the basement of their home so he could at least work there at night. He did, but when the children got to the age where their noise and activity bothered him, he would pack his bulging briefcase and go back to the office.

Over the years the company prospered and grew until it employed over 1,500 people. Al was promoted to the vice-presidency of engineering. Though he now had capable assistants to whom he could have delegated much of his work, his old habits of chronic overtime persisted.

In the meantime, his son had grown up and rejected that part of his father's life that made Dad the stranger who came home from the office only to sleep. Al's son got poor marks in high school and resented Al's urging that he prepare for college to the point where he swore at his father and spent a year working in a gas station. Ultimately the son realized the advantages of a college education, reconciled with Al, and went to Al's alma mater.

During the first week of a management-training seminar centered around feedback to each individual, Al was able to think through his workaholic life-style. Deciding he was going to work overtime only in extreme emergencies, he went back to his desk with the determination to delegate responsibility and to better manage his own time.

He did this so successfully that by the time the second week of the seminar came up a few months later, he could report to members of the group that he was managing in a totally different, much more satisfying way. He was getting much more out of life personally and feeling ten years younger as his job overload and stresses declined. Furthermore, Al's two very competent assistants were getting infinitely more job satisfaction, and Al had much more time to work with the president on long-range planning.

Managers born in the 1920s and 1930s were particularly trained to accept the work-ethic philosophy of living, which

holds that a person is worthwhile only when he is actively productive in his job. As a result, mid-career managers tend to be
particularly influenced by the organizational and social approval
that is given to the extremely hard-working manager. A manager
in today's society can work to the point of becoming a workaholic and still be seen as an extremely conscientious, even dedicated, member of his organization.

Many of the mid-career manager's stresses are a result of
his intense competitive strivings and preoccupation with his work.
In mid-career he often wakes up with a start to find that:

□ His children have grown up and left home without his
having given them as much time and attention as he would have
liked to.

□ These same children often reject his work-ethic values.
Like so many of their peers, they long for an ideal world where
being pleasant and likable will automatically lead to a rewarding
and interesting life free of stress and strain. Products of an affluent
society, they feel that their father's efforts and strivings have not
been worthwhile.

□ Although their mid-career-manager father may resent
some of these changing values and attitudes, he usually agrees
with at least part of the unfolding value and attitudinal changes
that our society has brought. This partial agreement causes him
to further question some of his own key personal values and as-
sumptions and to ask himself, "What's it all about?" Such ques-
tioning, doubt, or uncertainty can create a nagging stress in his
mind as he works at sorting out his own needs and goals in mid-
career.

□ His wife, bored with housework and the routines of child-
rearing, often wants either to develop a career of her own or to
get more deeply involved in hobbies or other interests as she
herself reaches mid-life. Often the manager has to re-examine the
quality and depth of his relationship with his wife now that the
children are leaving home. He has become so preoccupied with
his work and she with her child-rearing that the two have to
rework and rediscover their own interpersonal relationship in a
marriage that is again becoming a two-person unit.

□ For the manager as an individual, mid-career often brings him face to face with some of his own conflicting needs and goals. Up to this point he has typically been preoccupied with uncomfortably lopsided life-style as a result of his strenuous advancement and achievement. Both are essentially forms of proving oneself in competition with contemporaries.

Mid-career is a time when most managers have tangible proof of their material and social success. Settled in suburbia with its crabgrass, power mowers, snow blowers, bicycles, motor scooters, and two-car garages piled high with material goods, how can they doubt that they have "made it" in material terms?

But mid-life can be a particularly stressful time if the manager is overly concerned about declining physical vigor, about the increasing number of technically trained younger managers who report to him in the organization, or about having built an emphasis on work accomplishment.

THE MAN WHO SAID "I'M NOT YOUNG ANYMORE"

Bill represents the mid-career manager whose self-image and self-esteem are largely centered in his physical strength and skill, in addition to his personal enjoyment of winning in competitive sports. In business life Bill was the successful corporate vice-president in charge of a key staff function. His company had merged with a larger firm. Bill was regarded as a high-potential executive by the new owners. Insofar as his managerial career was concerned, he had made it and had done extremely well.

In sharing his personal feelings and concerns in a management seminar, Bill flatly came out and stated: "I'm not young anymore." He was concerned about the fact that it was difficult for him to keep pace with younger men in the competitive sport in which he had excelled in college. In fact, he recalled a three-man race in which he had recently competed with his own 20-year-old son, who was on a college team in Bill's favorite sport, and also with a third fellow about his son's age. Bill was extremely pleased that he had come in second in the race. But he also had guilt feelings about his own hostile feelings toward his son as a sports adversary during that race.

As a manager, Bill seems to have few job worries. In fact, in the business sense, he is an outstanding example of a successful manager and executive. If Bill wants to adjust his personal perceptions to the realities of his physiological limitations and thereby stop torturing himself about his declining athletic capabilities, he will have to see and appreciate himself for what he is now. Bill can engage in competitive sports and enjoy them if this continues to be of great psychological value to him. However, if he persists in chasing after the rainbow of his lost youth and continues to be upset because he can no longer compete with the 20-year-olds, he is apt to pay an unreasonable price in impractical longings and unrealistic regrets.

MID-CAREER: CRISIS OR OPPORTUNITY?

For the manager whose personal life-style pattern involves a heavy emphasis on competitive individual achievement, mid-life often presents some special problems. However, this does not mean that all managers must go through a deep and serious crisis when they reach their middle years. Some of the recent literature implies that this period must necessarily be full of crises.

The self-analysis tools provided in later chapters of this book will enable the manager to analyze his personal mid-career balance sheet. On the basis of this analysis he can take intelligent and constructive action to solve problems that confront him during this period. The self-analysis exercises can also be an aid in preventing significant problems from developing.

The practice of management by definition involves analytical approaches to problems. It also uses positive-action planning to work one's way out of the many crises that come up on the job. So the reader-manager already possesses the basic tools necessary to look constructively at where he has been up to this point in his life and career; what reasonable options are available to him at this stage; and what realistic things he can do now that will give him the greatest probability of having a good life in the future.

This is not to say that the middle years are without emotional stresses, doubts, or uncertainties. All people have some problems in this period. For many of us, oriented toward work primarily at the problem-solving level, self-analysis is a new experience. It may be somewhat uncomfortable if we have to do a lot of changing to match up our hopes and ambitions with realities that fall short of our dreams. It may also require us to adjust our self-image and our mid-life behavior to the new physiological, sociological, and psychological realities of our present world. Looking at our life-style and admitting that work preoccupations have caused an imbalance in our interpersonal relationships and our community commitments means that we have to be honest with ourselves. We may also find that we have neglected even our own hobbies and interests. As all managers know, however, crises do not arise from realistic anticipation and planning. They occur through lack of it. They also develop when we are not realistic in examining the facts of a situation. Not taking necessary steps at the right time also causes difficulties.

MID-LIFE: WHAT'S IT ALL ABOUT?

Mid-life is simply a fact indicating one has lived a certain portion of one's total life span. As the very young World War II American Air Force colonel replied to the British matron who asked him in astonishment how he could possibly have acquired such a high rank at such an obviously early age, "I just kept on livin', ma'am."

Since mid-life managers have "kept on livin'" to this particular point in their life span, they are now, by definition, middle-aged. Middle age, in our youth-oriented, consumer-wooed society, means that we have to face certain physiological, sociological, and psychological facts of life. For example, we do not have the same amount of energy and drive that we had in our teens and twenties. If we decide not to look at mid-life realistically, we tend to rationalize and pretend that things are other than they really are. This avoidance can make it harder to face problems later on when they reach a critical stage.

Here are some key influences that become important to consider.

Physiological Aspects

For most managers, mid-life brings an inevitable decline in physical energy and reserves. The manager who could work around the clock for long periods now finds that he has to slow down or run the risk of a heart attack, ulcers, insomnia, chronic fatigue, and possibly periods of emotional depression. The hard-charger type of manager, who places great emphasis on physical vigor and inexhaustible energy reserves, is the type most apt to be hard hit by the physiological decline associated with mid-life. Since his entire life-style has been built on the assumption that his energy reserves will go on forever, feeling tired or being unable to push himself as long as he used to makes him anxious. Many managers have become so preoccupied with work activity that they don't take time to develop a systematic physical exercise program. Such a program can minimize the sags and spreads that typically come with mid-life. More and more business organizations now sponsor exercise classes on company time. These classes use company-provided equipment and are held under supervision of the company medical staff.

Well-developed physical exercise programs can do much to reduce the internal pressures that often confront the manager in mid-career. Not knowing how to slow down or how to lead a more balanced life, many become resentful when the body will no longer obey the commands of their drives and ambitions. As many managers have come to realize, weekend golf or a few strenuous sets of tennis with the neighbors is insufficient. It is not an adequate substitute for regular, planned exercise.

Mid-career is also the time when minor physical ailments or debilities can develop. They may force us to alter our former "inexhaustible" way of life. Someone once said that the best prescription for longevity is to "develop a minor ailment early in life and then to adjust one's life-style to it." But anything that smacks of declining physical vigor and stamina is often greeted with apprehension and dismay by the manager when he becomes middle-aged.

Sociological Aspects

Our youth culture, with advertising's overwhelming emphasis on the vibrant, vital, animated teen-ager and under-30 adult, makes the person in mid-life feel that he has indeed crossed over into senility when he reaches 35. Since our society is geared to youthful images, mid-life seems to be an unpleasantly early termination of much that is glorious, glamorous, and exciting.

In television commercials and newspaper and magazine advertising, youth is seen as the glorious age when people love, laugh, have fun, do exciting and daring things, and "live life to the full." Mid-life, on the other hand, is seen as a period when our aches and pains can only be soothed by special liniments and elixirs. Youth-oriented novels portray mid-life as a period of sober responsibilities, personal disillusionments, often frayed and broken dreams, and unsatisfactory interpersonal relations.

Television soap operas in particular wallow in the disappointments, crises, confusions, and anguish of the middle-aged. In the soaps, women in mid-life usually strive for romance that never was or that passed them by in their youth. Male characters in such dramas always find their lives filled with horrendous complications on the job, in the home, and with their neighbors.

It is difficult for the manager not to be influenced by such a barrage from the media implying that to be middle-aged is to be painfully over the hill. The diminished enjoyment they portray carries over into the individual's private world of self-images and expectations. As a consequence, the first minor twinges, aches, and strains of mid-life are apt to be taken as harbingers of inevitable decline, decay, and doom.

Psychological Aspects

The combination of physiological realities and contemporary sociological role images and stereotypes put needless psychological pressures on the manager when he reaches mid-career. Anyone who has survived the trials and tribulations of adolescence—the most awkward of times—should be able to adjust to middle age with relative ease and comfort. However, a person at this stage of life has to consider several aspects of his life if he is to cope effectively with the problems and stresses that usually arise.

Despite inferences that the mid-career period is inevitably full of gloom and hardship, it *can* be a fruitful and rewarding life stage. At this point the manager often reaches a new peak in terms of knowledge, experience, and judgment. By bringing these three resources to bear on his personal situation, the individual can come through this period not only with humor and a positive perspective but also with an increased sense of self-worth and accomplishment. In doing this he can get more gratification from all aspects of his life including work, love, and leisure time.

2/Mid-Career and the Job

IN OUR complex industrial society, most of us are known by the kind of work we do; thus work plays a central part in our lives. This chapter and Chapters 3 through 6 will examine four major facets of the work world: the job, the organization, work relationships with associates, and career and personal development.

The kind of work we do affects our overall social status. Our salary and organizational positions are translated into community and neighborhood social position. It also influences our feelings of self-worth insofar as this relates to adult behavior and to demonstrations of competence as a mature individual. People generally rank jobs in social terms with regard to their relative status and desirability. The professions, industrial management, education, and the arts and entertainment fields are usually considered relatively high-status jobs.

THE CAREER

We build our careers over a working lifetime by performing a series of job assignments within organizational settings. A career is thus the sum total of a person's work experiences up to any given point in time. Some individuals move up the promotional ladder rapidly. Such fast-track individuals have to acquire the necessary expertise to do each new job adequately. If they have serious deficiencies in abilities, capacities, or skills, they run the risk of failure. Even if they do not fail completely, the knowledge that they are not really capable of handling assignments effectively creates a psychological strain for most managers. Outright failure, of course, usually brings a downward turn in one's life-career pattern.

Other managers find that they move up the ladder for a time and then their jobs plateau out. Advancement opportunities either cease or slow down markedly. If a manager's job-promotion level roughly equals his personal ambitions, he is apt to be happy and satisfied with himself. But when the gap between the manager's career attainment level and his career ambitions is marked and obvious by the time he reaches mid-career, he is apt to be unhappy—even despondent. His job, the organization, probably future opportunities, and even his estimation of self-worth all take on a negative coloration.

In some career situations, fast-track-promotion managers are moved along too rapidly for their own good. Eventually they reach a point where the gap between their capabilities and the job demands of higher-level positions becomes too great. When this happens, they usually run into difficulty. If this happens in mid-career, the manager may find himself under a particularly stressful set of pressures. Charlie is an example of such a manager.

A SERIES OF FAST-TRACK PROMOTIONS
THAT BROUGHT MID-CAREER DIFFICULTY

Being on a fast-track promotion path in a growth organization is one of the most stimulating experiences that can befall an ambitious young manager. Such a situation, however, sometimes carries the potential problems of *burnout* and *overpromotion*. These will be discussed in detail later.

Charlie is an example of a manager on a fast-track promotion pattern who ran into mid-career difficulties. Having had a limited formal education, he nevertheless possessed good skills in dealing with people and a warm desire to meet the goals set by his bosses. These characteristics enabled him to move rapidly up the operations route during his fifteen years with the company.

At one point a reorganization meeting was held in which the company president tentatively offered Charlie the vice-presidency of operations for the whole organization. During the discussion that followed, the board chairman, the president, two key vice-presidents, and an outside consultant reviewed Charlie's skills and his capacity to handle this job. The proposed assignment was of special significance for the future of the entire company.

The consultant argued that it was not in Charlie's best long-range career interests to take on this responsibility at this particular time. A strong point against his moving into the position was the fact that Charlie's key assistants had all been promoted very rapidly. Therefore, they had limited ability to give him strong back-up support.

Though it hurt his ego, Charlie agreed to take an assignment at the next level down in operations. Over the next two years, the company installed a number of relatively sophisticated new systems for long-range planning, management by objectives, and performance appraisal. Requirements of the new systems, plus further organizational growth, forced Charlie to manage primarily through paperwork, meetings, and phone conversations. He did not have as much time as he used to for the face-to-face contacts that had been the keystone of his managerial success in previous years.

Charlie, unfortunately, did not take the time to improve his skills in decision making and in administrative management during this phase of his career, though he was urged to do so by his boss. Had he done so, it is possible he could have better handled the new job and continued his career upward. Because of the increasing gap between job requirements and his capabilities, he soon began to show obvious signs of having difficulty in managing his new responsibilities.

As things got worse, his relationships with his boss, the hard-charging president of the company, became more strained. His performance-appraisal reviews became more negative. The president finally decided that he would have to go outside the company and hire an additional operating executive. This man had demonstrated his profit-making ability in a very large division of a competing company.

At this mid-career point Charlie was faced with a *bypassing situation*. (This concept is discussed in detail later.) He was given the choice of remaining at his current job level with the same salary and stock benefits or resigning. Feeling that he had not been given an adequate chance to prove himself in the assignment, Charlie took the resignation option.

This choice does not mean that Charlie's career is completely stymied—indeed, he may well go on to bigger things in another growth organization. But both Charlie and his original company lost because he was unable to make the required managerial transitions successfully.

CLIMBING THE JOB-STATUS LADDER

By the time most managers reach mid-career they usually have had a series of progressively more responsible job assignments. Typically the individual starts out at a beginning level, often working in his area of technical specialization, if he has one. Thus he begins his organizational work life as an accountant, a plant engineer, a salesman, a computer specialist, or the like.

In the past, and probably for many mid-career managers today, progression up the job-status ladder took some time. Between 1950 and 1970, rapid career advancement was quite commonplace for those who worked in fast-track promotional situations. For most managers, though, it was less rapid; in the 1950s a man expected to spend from two to five or more years at a given job level before moving up.

Since the mid-1960s a generation of technically trained young engineers and business school graduates has entered organizational life. A high proportion moved up the position advancement ladder at a significantly rapid rate. Their specialized training, plus the manpower requirements resulting from national and international organization expansion, brought many of them into fast-track advancement situations.

SPECIALIST OR MANAGER? A DIFFICULT CHOICE

Organizational advancement and reward are more frequently associated with managing than with remaining in a technical specialty. For the ambitious person, the choice between staying in his specialty or moving up the management ladder is a difficult one. The latter path is likely to bring him more power, recognition, status, and monetary reward. Most men who aspire to advance take this route even though it means giving up the alternative satisfaction of being a highly competent individual performer.

Because the nature of managerial work is different from that of the individual specialist, taking the management path is likely to have some discomforts. Typically the competent and successful salesman is offered a promotion to first-level sales management as a reward for his accomplishments. The managerial job brings *extrinsic* rewards in terms of status, pay, and power. But it may not give the born salesman the *intrinsic* satisfactions related to customer contact and high individual sales performance that he finds so personally rewarding.

The ego satisfaction he got in making the big sale or in customer interaction does not exist for him as a manager. Instead, his time is spent in supervising district salesmen or getting urgent deliveries from the factory. Or he may find that he spends a large part of his day with his managerial superiors discussing sales and marketing strategies. He may not particularly enjoy the intricacies and pressures associated with the management job into which he has been promoted.

Some mid-career men make the transition from technical specialist to manager with relative ease. Others have a more difficult time. Dave is a manager who finds his regional sales job to be currently stressful because of a variety of internal organizational pressures. On the other hand, Ernie, a former research scientist, has grown to be quite comfortable with his managerial assignment. It involves his serving as liaison manager between the research lab and the corporate marketing group.

A Regional Sales Manager with Intra-Organizational Difficulties

Dave, a regional sales manager for a large organization, finds his attempts to deal with the corporate product managers, who are graduates of top business schools, to be frustrating and disturbing. Dave's job is to supervise a crew of field salesmen engaged in obtaining maximum product exposure and sales for their company's products. His company markets through retail distributors who also sell competing private and national-label brands.

Dave knows his job well. He has an excellent practical education and knows how to get results in the field. His difficulties mount when he attempts to influence the business-school-trained product managers. These men are specialists at corporate headquarters who give him the promotional and other dollar support he needs for his particular products.

The specialist product managers treat Dave and his fellow regional sales managers like second-class citizens. Dave enjoys being out in the field—selling and directing field salesmen. But he finds more and more of his time has to be spent in planning meetings with the product managers. In these meetings many of his suggestions and recommendations are either brushed aside or ignored.

Much of Dave's time is spent writing memos and replying to requests for corporate surveys that are unlikely ever to be used. He feels he is being second-guessed by some "textbook genius" for whatever actions he takes in the field. The product managers, it seems to Dave, are full of business school theory but would have real difficulty in performing a regional sales manager's job if they were transferred to field operations. In this situation, Dave is inclined to become a philosopher. He does his job to the best of his ability and tries to protect his own subordinates from the criticisms and pressures that staff experts generate.

The Technical Specialist Who Went into a Marketing Liaison Job

Ernie is a mid-career manager who left his primary interests—industrial research and research management—to fill an important void on the company's marketing staff. He spent a number of years getting his doctorate in his research specialty. During that time he was promoted from a researcher to a supervisor. After receiving the doctor's degree he was further promoted to laboratory manager. Eventually he became director of research in the company's largest research laboratory.

A few years later, corporate management asked him to leave research and research management to take a new job as research liaison manager with the headquarters marketing group. This new position was created so that the lab's research output could be more carefully evaluated for possible use. Without a research man like Ernie in this position, the gap between research and marketing was too great, and many potentially worthwhile projects had never been carried to completion. Also, through lack of understanding, marketing often failed to give advertising and sales support for new products that required special assistance.

For Ernie, the new marketing liaison job required a considerable personal adjustment. Trained to think along scientific lines, he often found the subjective, impressionistic, emotionally oriented marketing types he worked with at corporate headquarters to be both baffling and frustrating—especially when he tried to communicate with them about the technical merits of some new products. He has, however, grown reasonably comfortable in his new world. He has also become a more successful "salesman" in terms of getting corporate budget support for highly technical projects that top corporate managers do not understand well. Even though he misses some of the satisfactions he found in research management, Ernie's trade-off choice in his job change has come out on the plus side.

JOB STATUS AND SELF-ESTEEM

Most mid-career managers today probably started up the technical route and shifted at some point into managerial work. The typical American manager habitually puts a great percentage of his waking time and effort into work performance and career achievement. His job responsibility and accomplishment are tied in with his sense of self-worth and ego satisfaction.

When businessmen meet, they typically communicate "who they are" by exchanging information about their work. "What kind of work are you in?" is both a factual question and a way of finding out about the other's relative social status. When the other person says, "I'm a manager in X company," he implies that he has reached a certain station in life. He may also be indicating that his job involves him in the administrative details and organizational pressures associated with being a manager in a certain type of organization at a certain responsibility level.

JOB STRESS AND ADJUSTMENT

Membership in an organization's top management group does not guarantee the mid-career manager that his sense of self-worth and his ego gratifications relating to job performance will be secure from then on. Executive life in certain companies in the aerospace, communications, transportation, computer, autonomative, and food industries has been anything but a bed of roses during the past few years, as Joel Ross and Michael Cami write in *Corporate Management in Crisis*. Nor have some of the conglomerates fared much better.

Pressures Vary with Levels of Management

Being a member of top management in some of these organizations at the mid-career point may even produce a peculiar set of headaches. Unless the individual has wide ability to market his skills elsewhere if the need arises, his high position plus his salary, stock options, and bonus arrangements may tend to lock him into one type of job—and even into one company. If that happens, he is almost forced to sink or swim, career-wise, with his organization. Even though he does not control its direction or its ultimate success, his personal world is very much tied up with what is happening to it.

Middle-level managers have different sets of work-career problems. These usually result from pressures for short-run operating results that top management places upon them. They also get pressured by lower-level management and by hourly employees in the form of union contract provisions. These may closely regulate what the middle manager can and cannot do in decision making. Some union contracts are virtual straitjackets in which the mid-career manager is forced to operate as best he can.

First-level managerial pressures result from the firing-line nature of their jobs. One chronic headache results from the never-ending pressure to get production or service deliveries out to customers on a tight time-and-cost schedule. For many first-line managers, life is a never-ending struggle against deadlines, equipment limitations, breakdowns, malfunctions, and intra-organizational demands.

Because of the pressure-cooker quality of this level of managerial work, misunderstandings, resentments, and interpersonal misperceptions abound. The first-line manager in mid-career may find that both his physical stamina and personal flexibility decline. He becomes more testy and short-tempered and feels put upon much of the time. As Shakespeare would put it, his ability to "withstand the slings and arrows of outrageous fortune" decreases at this life stage.

High-Stress Aspects of Managerial Work

In organizations where crisis management or manipulative power plays are the order of the day, the mid-career manager may feel like the canoeist who has been riding the rapids of a swirling, churning river for too long. He gets tired of paddling just to keep the canoe afloat, and any bend in the river might throw him out of the canoe. When one has been subjected to a series of job strains and stresses over a long period of time, it is difficult to maintain a positive sense of self-worth and a firm ego identity. Yet for most managers, managerial work inherently contains a substantial element of never-ending pressures.

One of the dangers of continuous job pressures is the possibility of becoming accustomed to working with a high adrenalin output. The manager may have his body chemistry so adjusted to pressure that it chronically produces a high level of adrenalin. Nature designed this to help individuals meet primitive crises and emergencies. When a person gets into relatively relaxing, calm, unpressured situations, his adrenalin does not flow at the same rate. The sense of excitement associated with flight or fight preparation is then gone. But to some managers, this appears to be an overly tame and uninteresting work climate and emotional state. Individuals who compulsively drive themselves to perform more and more work in less and less time may eventually reach a point where they become prime candidates for coronary difficulties.

Job Stress and Psychological Pressure

Job pressures for some mid-career managers eventually reach the level where they produce chronic physiological problems. Situations that generate high job-stress levels include crisis management, anxiety about one's ability to handle his job adequately, and habitual overloads of one sort or another. Stresses resulting from competition or from being outside organizational power situations also take their toll. Sharp differences in styles and values among managers whose work requires close interaction can cause stress; and having to make difficult decisions without adequate data or without the ability to predict consequences creates additional pressures.

Some managers become so accustomed to handling chronic work overloads or tasks with high inherent stresses that they come to think of themselves as "Mr. Troubleshooter." Frank is an example of a mid-career manager who was beginning to suffer physical difficulties as a result of filling this role for many years in his company.

Mr. Troubleshooter

Frank's case is an interesting one of a man whose managerial career consisted largely of getting himself involved in complicated, difficult, and draining troubleshooting assignments. A technical specialist, he started out in the troubleshooting aspects of quality control some 20 years ago. In his industry, zero-defects quality control is crucial because of the nature of the products. Mistakes are very costly.

Frank grew accustomed to wearing the troubleshooter label, and the organization automatically turned to him to solve very difficult problems. Psychologically and physiologically, his job stresses built up over the years. Eventually they took a physical toll. He developed metabolic problems as well as heart and blood-pressure difficulties in his mid-40s. Unfortunately, no one in the organization, least of all Frank himself, ever thought of reducing the stresses under which he typically operated.

As he discussed these job pressures and his overall life-style in a management seminar, fellow group members asked him point-blank why he felt he had to carry this strenuous burden on his shoulders. They suggested that he consider letting his three young assistants handle at least some of these special projects. It had simply never occurred to Frank, because he had seen himself as Mr. Troubleshooter for such a long time, that he could and should delegate more of the pressure aspects of his job to key assistants.

By the time the second management session rolled around some months later, Frank was happy to report that his assistants, each highly competent and personally ambitious, were "eating up this new delegation." (One of them had formerly contemplated asking for a transfer because he had felt Frank wasn't giving him enough challenging work to do.) Frank's blood pressure had dropped to near normal, and he was finding more time for his hobbies and interests. His general tension level was sharply reduced. Had he not made this change in his work life at mid-career, he might have been "invalided out" of the company in a relatively few years. Continued physical stresses would almost certainly have resulted in serious physical impairment.

Decision-Making Stresses

Many organizations place a premium on managerial decision making of the sort that involves neither high risks nor the possibility of making serious errors. A particular problem for the mid-career manager in today's high-technology organization occurs when he has to rely on the judgments and recommendations of technical specialists whose suggestions he is unable to check fully. If he lacks expertise in their special skill area, he must accept their recommendations. Some such recommendations can be quantitatively checked out in terms of their probable soundness. Unfortunately many managerial decisions have qualitative aspects that are difficult to put into probability ratios. Even some well-thought-out decisions might go wrong over time when changes in external or internal organizational circumstances arise without warning.

If the line manager is seen as relying too much on staff technical specialists for advice, his peers and superiors may assume that he lacks self-confidence. Should he develop some actual self-doubts about his own decision making, they see him as having lost the decisiveness required to be an effective manager.

The ebb and flow of organizational priorities makes it difficult to be certain that one's decisions will be viewed in hindsight as having been organizationally correct. For example, cost reduction may be the most important criterion for making decisions when an organization is in a profit slide. The criterion may shift abruptly to that of spending money to gear for rapid expansion when business takes an upturn. Sometimes top management fails to signal clearly at which point the manager ought to shift his decision-making criterion from cost consciousness to expansion spending. Those managers who do not correctly anticipate the early warning signals of such shifts are seen as being out of step with the organization's new direction. Consequently their decision-making abilities are questioned.

**Psychological Adjustments to Externally
Imposed Job Changes**

An important skill of the successful mid-career manager is the ability to adjust to externally imposed changes in his work situation. Often he has little direct control over such changes as acquisitions and mergers and rapid increases or decreases in organizational growth or profitability. Reorganizations involve getting used to new bosses, new responsibilities, and new job requirements. The manager's duties are frequently modified to the point where he has to make a significant personal readjustment to the new situation in order to function effectively. For the mid-career manager, continual reorganization may call for more psychological flexibility than he possesses.

SELECTED READINGS

Joel Ross and Michael Cami, *Corporate Management in Crisis: Why the Mighty Fall* (Englewood Cliffs, N.J.: Prentice-Hall, 1973).
Meyer Friedman, M.D., and Ray Rosenmann, M.D., *Type A Behavior and Your Heart* (New York: Knopf, 1974).

3/Work Life

IN OUR COMPLEX, organizationally structured society, most of us work within an organizational framework. Relatively few independent entrepreneurs and some professionals work largely on a one-man basis. Nevertheless, they have to have support personnel to assist them: typists, file clerks, accountants, assistants, secretaries, nurses, receptionists, and so on.

Organizations may be small, similar to the two-dentist clinic with its supporting technician and bookkeeper-secretary. Or they may be large, like a giant corporation or a huge federal governmental agency. The interaction and teamwork required in larger organizations are naturally more complicated than those of the very small ones. But the basic organizational principles of planning, coordinating, motivating, and controlling employee behavior to reach organizational objectives are the same.

ORGANIZATIONAL CLIMATE

Organizational climate is a composite of top management's philosophies, strategies, and practices. Some organizations use broad responsibility delegation as a way of life. They also encourage freedom of action on a profit-center basis. Others are centrally controlled by the headquarters staff to the point of domination.

Some companies are fast-moving and growth-oriented. They continually seek new and more effective methods of getting organizational work done. Other organizations are inherently slow to change and bound by tradition. They set about doing everything in a precise and rigid manner.

Organizational climate has a strong influence on the types of people who are hired and who eventually get promoted to higher levels. Depending upon the type of organizational climate in which the mid-career manager finds himself, his work contribution could be highly valued or nearly ignored. In one type of organization he might be considered highly effective and worthy of praise, promotions, and pay increases. In another, his same performance could be relatively devalued, largely ignored, and sometimes even "punished" in the sense of lack of pay increases or advancements.

People-Using versus People-Building

Those organizations which treat their employees at all levels—except possibly the very top level—as they treat nonhuman aspects of the firm can be called *people-using*. People are seen in the same light as machines, materials, and equipment; little consideration or thought is given to human needs. "Produce or perish" is the unstated personnel philosophy of this type of organization. Employees are expected to produce; the paycheck is assumed to meet their individual needs.

People-building organizations are just beginning to flourish in our society. They are becoming increasingly concerned with the needs and aspirations of employees as individuals. The employee's contribution to organizational goals is considered a matter of personal motivation rather than an impersonal one that can be fully compensated for by money.

Adjusting to Changing Organizational Climates in Mid-Career

American organizations tend to be of three varieties. The *entrepreneurial* organization is the one-man-show type, dominated by the founder. The *bureaucratic* organization is the (usually large) one run by a centralized systems-and-policies group with tight control. Conformity to organizational behavioral expectations and demands is essential to survival in this kind of company. Since about 1950, a number of entrepreneurial and bureaucratic organizations have made strenuous efforts to move in the direction of *professional management.* The professionally managed organization is characterized by effective long-range planning, marketing orientation, management by objectives, and an overall *people-building philosophy.* Human resources are seen as crucial to organizational survival and growth.

The mid-career manager is often caught in a shift in his own organization away from the entrepreneurial or bureaucratic organization toward professional management. He needs to make a corresponding change in his own managerial techniques to effectively fit into the new climate situation.

For example, if a successful entrepreneur, who formerly made all the decisions in his organizations, introduces professional management techniques, his subordinates have to learn a new way of doing things. When the entrepreneur becomes more involved in planning, delegating, and managing by objectives than he formerly did, those under him are expected to take more initiative.

Most significant organizational climate changes are not achieved rapidly. Often the company shifts back and forth between the old philosophies and practices and the new. This continues over a period of years until the new programs become installed as a way of life. To do his job well in such transitional states, the mid-career manager has to be sensitive to the nuances of their ebb and flow.

In some organizations, two opposing groups of top managers form during these transition periods. One group, the *traditionalists,* would like to continue on in the old ways as long as possible. They feel uncomfortable with new methods and often lapse into their old accustomed patterns.

The second group, the *innovators,* want to experiment with new methods and philosophies in the hope of reaching long-term improvements in profits and growth. They push the organization to accept new techniques that, in our time, usually involve innovative planning, delegating, marketing, and human resources development methods.

As long as these climate transitions are consistent and orderly, the mid-career manager's own psychological and behavioral adjustments are not difficult. He gets reinforcement in the form of encouragement from the innovators to learn new behavior patterns. Unfortunately, in some organizational situations the traditionalist-innovator clashes take on the proportions of civil war. A most difficult mid-career stress situation arises when the manager gets caught directly in the crossfire between the two groups in corporate headquarters. This frequently happens to an area sales manager or plant manager when competing corporate groups each insist that the manager function their way. It is impossible for him to meet the conflicting demands of both groups. Nor is it easy for him to remain neutral. Deciding how to act to keep his work unit reasonably productive in such situations creates headaches for the man in the middle.

The Plant Manager Caught Between the Traditionalists and the Innovators

George is a mid-career manager whose job stresses were compounded by his position between traditionalist and innovator groups in his corporate headquarters. Years ago, George's father had been manager of the same plant that George currently runs. A small-town boy, George went to a local college and majored in industrial engineering. He has a good reputation as a technical plant manager and is liked by most of the employees in the plant. They view him as an understanding and people-oriented boss.

Corporate headquarters was divided into two distinct power groups. The traditionalists, who enjoyed wheeling and dealing in sales and purchasing, wanted to operate the company on a centralized control basis. Since headquarters is some three hundred miles away from the plant George manages, distance complicated his successful communication with these groups. The traditionalists let George know that he could keep his job as long as he follows their orders. George had gotten used to this situation; in fact, he functioned quite well within this framework.

The second group, the innovators, pushed hard to get the organization to adopt newer management techniques. Their version of these techniques included participative management, management by objectives, and individualized goal setting. George and the plant people also got encouragement from the innovators to do two-way problem solving with staff groups in corporate headquarters.

For a time the traditionalists went along with this new way of managing. They wanted to tell their industry peers that they were using the latest and most modern techniques. In addition, they were anxious to get whatever increased productivity and profits might come their way.

But when it came to actually listening to the problems the plant people brought up in their relations with the corporate staff, the traditionalists became indignant. Entrepreneurs among them resented the notion that they ought to be more logical and results-oriented in company planning. This took away the fun of their wheeling and dealing on the basis of spontaneous opportunity. The bureaucrats among them resented being told that their systems and production control methods were producing very poor plant production schedules.

Fortunately for George's situation, the innovator group declined in power at this juncture. The traditionalists took over again, making it clear that they wanted to go back to the old way of managing. George accepted this decision with a sigh of relief. The plant currently operates much as it did when his father was manager many years ago. Corporate headquarters changes signals on short notice. It also gets enmeshed in reams of paperwork, much of it computer generated. The plant is a lot less efficient. However, George's ulcers have quieted down because he is no longer pressured by the conflicting managerial philosophies of the two opposing groups.

WORK LIFE IN THE BUREAUCRATIC ORGANIZATION

The majority of today's mid-career managers find themselves working in organizations that are essentially bureaucratic in nature. These are characterized by a definite and rigid formal structure and planning based more on the historical past than on the competitive present and future, and are comprised of a series of interlocking subsystems (functional departments) bound together by intricate coordinating mechanisms.

Many bureaucratic organizations appear to the casual observer to run with the smooth efficiency of a well-oiled watch. Closer examination of such an organization's inner workings, however, often reveals complicated, redundant, and inefficient meshing of organizational components. The management development department of one large bureaucracy, for example, has to get a sign-off approval resembling a pontifical blessing from ten different division heads and staff groups in order to obtain authorization to give a three-day training seminar for 40 sales managers.

Bureaucratic organizations reached their full flower from 1900 to 1960. During this time many became large, complex, and relatively successful. Some still employ hundreds of thousands of employees. Their organizational advantages include resource consolidation plus highly specialized divisions of labor. In the process of evolving, some of these organizations have become more concerned with self-perpetuation and maintenance of the status quo than with adapting to a rapidly changing sociotechnical environment. Robert Blake and his associates have discussed this phenomenon in their studies on corporate Darwinism.

While many bureaucracies are still considered successful in terms of profit and current market share, many are actually relatively inefficient in today's high-technology society. The different types of career dilemmas mid-career managers confront in the bureaucratic organization illustrate many of the human-factor dilemmas faced by those who work in them.

The Seniority-Oriented Bureaucracy

Life proceeds at a slow and measured pace in the seniority-oriented bureaucracy. Its present-day managers were typically hired at starting levels after finishing high school or college. Many of them spent their entire working lives in the same organization. Such managers tend to get promoted as vacancies open up.

Success and advancement in this type of organization center around being a nice guy. Advancement comes from following the organizational rules of polite behavior to the letter. Above all, one should never rock the boat by seriously challenging the organizational system. Managers who possess average or below-average skills can still be promoted up to and sometimes beyond the vice-presidential level.

Centralized policy decision making is done only at the top level in low-technology organizations that are set up along bureaucratic lines. The system has a number of built-in safeguards to minimize deviation from central plan. Unfortunately, such checks and balances prevent much from getting done within a reasonable time frame. For example, one huge heavy-industry bureaucracy is said to require that a requisition for a $5,000 expenditure must pass through some 50 separate hands before final approval is given.

Mid-career managers who are ambitious and independent have difficulty fitting into the behavioral expectations of the seniority-oriented bureaucracy. Regardless of the results this type of manager may achieve, his associates are uncomfortable if he pushes too hard to get things done. On the other hand, the relaxed and affable mid-career manager may find life in this type of organization very congenial.

THE OFFICE BOY WHO BECAME VICE-PRESIDENT

Managers whose personalities fit comfortably into the seniority-oriented bureaucracy find life in such an organization agreeable—at least up to the point where their abilities and managerial style can no longer meet the higher-level requirements of the jobs into which they are ultimately promoted.

Harold is such a person. He literally started out as an office boy (this case is slightly dated but has its more modern counterparts in many contemporary bureaucracies). After he went to a commercial school and learned typing and shorthand, he accompanied the president on a number of business trips. Through these trips Harold met many people who liked him, while also acquiring knowledge of the company's key decisions and policies.

Over the years he was promoted, through sequential job levels, to vice-president of sales. His company's product was essential to certain types of heavy industry. There was little real competition from other organizations that produced the same product. Therefore Harold's sales activities consisted largely of helping to schedule deliveries. Occasionally he did some low-key general entertainment types of selling with executives in customer organizations.

While the corporation's headquarters remained in the town in which he was born and raised, and while his job was relatively simple in terms of managerial decision making, Harold did quite well. He was never particularly effective, and he always operated with a relatively high degree of nervous tension. But he got by. His personal amiability led others to overlook his occasional managerial blunders.

But when corporate headquarters moved to a large urban center and his job became more complex, he had obvious difficulty in managing. Soon he began to have physiological problems that were apparently induced by job stress. Fortunately, Harold had been with the company for over 30 years at that point, and he was able to take a graceful early retirement before his physical condition became too serious.

Had he been aware of the additional stresses that the move to the large city would likely impose, he might have negotiated with the company to stay at the lower-level job in his hometown. Such a career choice can be a good one for some mid-career managers. In such cases, both the individual and his organization gain by not trying to force him to accept a promotional situation that he is not equipped to handle.

The Manipulative-Oriented Bureaucracy

When bureaucratic organizations operate largely on the basis of personal likes and dislikes rather than on performance, their organizational climates become manipulative. In such organizations, politically oriented executives form power groups, which are sometimes used to protect the group's share of organizational benefits. At other times they become jumping-off points for the acquisition of even more power.

The individual's chances of being taken on as a member of one of these power groups is often based on ethnic, religious, and educational factors. Social class, geographical area of birth, and attendance at select schools are other factors that influence acceptance. David Halberstam gave detailed descriptions of the backgrounds of individuals in such groups in the federal government during the Kennedy–Johnson years. *Fortune* magazine entertainingly analyzed the Bunky Knudsen–Lee Iacocca power struggles in the Ford Motor Company when Knudsen left General Motors to become president of Ford.

In some manipulative bureaucracies, these groups operate in a manner resembling that of the Mafia families in *The Godfather*. Members of one group enter into power struggles with members of rival groups. The prize for the survivors is greater domination of organizational resources and policies.

Being in or out of a key power group has obvious consequences for the mid-career manager's future rewards and opportunities. Since the typical manipulative bureaucracy has no use for a management-by-objectives program, the individual's personal fortunes are closely tied to his place in the group power structure.

If he lacks the qualifications for full membership in such groups, his opportunities and rewards are automatically limited. He will inevitably get less choice assignments and fewer promotions. When reorganizations occur, he often finds his job has been moved laterally or downward in the status structure. More favored power group members are advanced over his head simply because they are "on the team."

Survival and possible advancement for the individual who is not a member of the controlling power group require a good deal of "maze brightness." Particularly in mid-career, the manager has to be keenly aware of how organizational influence and decision-making networks operate on an informal basis. He wants to avoid the pitfalls inherent in taking too vigorous a stand on the "wrong" side of key policy issues. Winding up on the wrong side can harm his career chances regardless of how correct or economically profitable his ideas may be.

The Techniques-Oriented Bureaucracy

Many bureaucratic organizations are currently in transition. With the adoption of new techniques for planning, forecasting, management by objectives, and the like, they are moving in the direction of professional management. In this transitional process, some organizations become stuck at a stage of arrested development, a situation in which the techniques-oriented bureaucracy places a great deal of emphasis on professional management techniques. But the organization uses them in a basically bureaucratic manner.

Top management sincerely espouses full utilization of professional management techniques, determined to reap the benefits it sees attached to them. It is further willing to invest considerable sums of money in setting up major programs that have a professional management theme. These often include management and organizational development, corporate planning related to manpower planning, and motivation in terms of carefully developed monetary and nonmonetary rewards. Many operating managers pay lip service to the new methods and systems, but they continue to run things in the same old bureaucratic way, as Alfred J. Marrow describes in *The Failure of Success*.

The mid-career manager who works in the bureaucracy that has fixated at the techniques-oriented stage finds himself living in two different worlds. The official word from top management says the company is to fully utilize enlightened contemporary techniques of planning, organizing, measuring, and motivating. But when the mid-career manager regards the situation objectively he finds a sharp gap between what top management professes and what his immediate superiors practice.

For example, one large corporation was a pioneer in setting up a corporate career-development department, moving far ahead of other firms in their industry in budgeting for this service. But when it came to finding a manager to fill this spot, they eventually decided upon a man who had been transferred from one staff-and-line job to another in a vain attempt to "find the right place for him." This manager is uninterested in career development. Moreover, he sees this job as another career sidetrack. As a consequence, the usable output from this department over the past few years has been nil.

In such organizations, the mid-career manager has to steer his career course between what top management *says* ought to be happening and what he actually *sees* going on about him. If he pays too much attention to top management's rhetoric, he will miss the fact that his immediate superiors do not intend to use the new methods any more than they have to.

Like his counterpart in the seniority-oriented bureaucracy, he can look forward to a comfortable career. If he is adequately trained in some functional area such as finance, accounting, marketing, engineering, or management and doesn't make too many major goofs, he can expect to reach middle, upper middle, and sometimes top management without any special effort on his part. This is particularly true when his company is in a growth situation.

His work world will have some minor stresses, usually in the form of manpower cutbacks, job assignment transfers, and occasional intergroup policy conflicts between units like sales and manufacturing. If, however, he sticks to the organizationally approved work role and uses the shiny new tools provided by top management in the old cautiously bureaucratic manner, he will complete his career in relative comfort. Retirement will bring excellent financial remuneration and benefits. In addition, his former job as a manager will entitle him to a considerable degree of status and prestige when he retires.

Avoiding the "Bureaucratic Blahs"

How to sidestep boredom in mid-career is a dilemma for the energetic and ambitious manager in the bureaucratic organization. If he has a reasonable track record and avoids getting on the losing end of power struggles, he will almost inevitably wind up with what the world regards as a comfortable and even an enviable career. Unfortunately there often comes a time when some successful mid-career managers get hit by the "bureaucratic blahs."

The Manager with the Bureaucratic Blahs

Irvin entered a management seminar appearing stooped and somber. At first glance he looked five or ten years older than his chronological age. Quiet and rather sad in appearance, he had little to say about anything at the first several meetings.

His career story is both simple and successful. He is plant manager of one of the largest and most productive processing plants in a high-technology field. The nature of the product required plant location in a rural mountainous area off the beaten track. Irvin has been in charge of this plant for eight very successful years. Periodically the vice-president of operations, a man very well satisfied with Irvin's performance, comes down from corporate headquarters. Occasionally other members of the corporate staff make brief inspection tours, mainly to enjoy the hunting and fishing that the area provides.

As plant manager, Irvin has the job running so well that he is seldom needed to make other than occasional decisions. His two capable younger assistants run the plant on a daily basis. He could, as he often does, take two or three hours off for lunch to play squash or handball in the local gym. His salary and bonuses advance each year. He is now one of the highest-paid plant managers in his industry with an excellent retirement program. He is liked and respected by all of his superiors in the company.

But in terms of his career ambitions, there is no place he can go in the near future. The corporate vice-president of operations and his assistant are both about Irv's age. The company is not currently expanding. All Irv has to look forward to is two to five more years in the same location. There is no other company in his industry that could give him a better job. Perhaps in two to five years his own organization will open a new plant. Then he can make a move.

Meanwhile, Irv sits at his desk. He reads reports, looks out the window, and sinks into a sort of genteel decline. There isn't enough to challenge or to stimulate him in his current work environment. His community and family relationships are pleasant but equally bland. During the past year he has become depressed at the lack of stimulation and challenge in life. Yet when he goes to his college alumni reunions, his envious classmates, who beat their brains out working in the big cities, tell him he "has it made," living as he does in exactly the type of place many of them rush to at vacation time.

In the management seminar, Irvin blossomed in response to the positive and supportive feedback he got from group members. They all expressed sincere admiration for him as a person and as a manager. If Irv could build on this positive experience, he could do much to recharge his personal enthusiasm on his own. To do this successfully he will have to learn how to bring interest and stimulation to the small town where he lives. He can do this through reading, through taking appropriate management training courses on an extension basis, or by becoming active in local and regional management and professional organizations. He can also schedule business trips to give him and his wife a few extra days' stop-off in interesting cities.

The bureaucratic blahs in Irvin's case result from being successful in a secure job in a large organization. (Unfortunately, this company lacks an effective human resources development program for its key managers.) There is really nothing for Irv to complain about strongly, yet he is unhappy because of the daily boredom and monotony that have settled into his life at mid-career. If he explores his own life-style and interests using the outlines in Chapters 9 and 10 in this book, he will find suggestions for setting up a self-directed change program.

The blahs are usually not themselves so overwhelming. The difficulty often lies in a lack of challenges coupled with a monotonous routine. The mid-career manager in such a situation finds that the walls are starting to close in on him, even though he is leading a comfortable life—in many ways a life that less fortunate associates and neighbors envy. If he feels he may have to go through another twenty or thirty years of much the same routine in the same type of job and organization, the future appears bleak. One consequence can be a type of depression—a feeling of futility and meaninglessness. Customary routines and daily managerial duties become burdensome. Insight into the causes of these feelings will help the mid-career manager to avoid sinking deeper into a rut.

In Irvin's case, his management course experience brought about a great deal of positive reassurance through feedback. This boost to his self-esteem encouraged him to take positive action to change his feelings and attitudes. Along with some specific life-style changes he can develop an entirely new and fresh approach to his mid-career situation.

WORK LIFE IN THE ENTREPRENEURIAL ORGANIZATION

Like bureaucracies, entrepreneurial organizations have several distinct types of subclimates. The climate that develops in any particular entrepreneurial firm depends largely upon the interests and skills of the founder. Professors Orvis Collins and David Moore have done a thorough study of the personality dynamics of typical entrepreneurs.

Some are basically salesmen. They enjoy wheeling and dealing. The climate in such organizations tends to reflect the hyperactive, negotiations-oriented style of the boss. Usually there is little organizational planning—everything centers around quick action in pursuit of short-range opportunities.

Most salesmen-entrepreneurs are enthusiastic promoters who sell continuously to their subordinates as well as to their customers. Fired with personal enthusiasm, the owner promises liberal bonuses and salary increases if subordinates work hard to help him succeed. Loyal followers eventually become disenchanted by the gap between his promises and reality unless the organization succeeds and the founder is really willing to share the success. The more able employees leave after such disenchantment. As a result, the firm run by a salesman-entrepreneur usually experiences much top staff turnover. The owner, who is often suspicious of others' motives, may take their departure as a personal affront. In turn, this can make him bitter and resentful. He seems unhappy when subordinates refuse to continue to accept his dreams and promises in lieu of cash.

Other entrepreneurs are basically engineers at heart. They are preoccupied with the technical aspects of the business—

machinery, systems, and processes. Such men spend their time getting personally involved in production, product development, and sometimes in research. Mid-career managers in such organizations find that much attention is given to product quality and to the organization's delivery system. But often not enough thought is given to organization building and financial planning.

As a consequence, the technically oriented entrepreneur often sells out to better-managed firms. He then takes his capital gains and starts another small, technically oriented firm. He then repeats this cycle in terms of his personal interests in the technical side of the organization. Managers who helped him build the initial firm sometimes find, in mid-career, that the company has been sold out from under them. At this point in their lives they then have to begin the arduous processes of rebuilding their personal career programs.

Still another type of entrepreneur founds an organization primarily as an extension of his own ego. He wants a vehicle for exercising his desire to dominate and control other people, like the strong, domineering, and often emotionally aggressive father in some families. These personality types get their greatest personal enjoyment from telling subordinates exactly what they must do. They also enjoy rewarding and punishing those beneath them in much the same way the authoritarian parent does when raising his children.

Managerial life in these organizations revolves around transactions between subordinates and the great man-founder as he acts out his aggressive needs. Subordinates adept at playing such games as those Eric Berne has described ("Kick Me," "Schlemiel," "Ain't It Awful," and "Look at What He Did Wrong") often find favor in the organization run by the dominance-oriented entrepreneur.

Evolution of Entrepreneurial Firms

Today's entrepreneurial firms usually fail and go under, evolve into a mixed entrepreneurial-bureaucratic type of organization, or emerge as a professionally managed company. Some of them shift back and forth between entrepreneurial and bureaucratic climates. They grow to a certain size, peak out because they lack the managerial skills needed to bring them farther along, then drop back to a smaller size and scope. This cycle may be repeated many times over the organization's life where the entrepreneurial founder lacks the managerial competence to build beyond the one-man-show type of organization, which can reach only a certain size.

The Struggling Entrepreneurship

Mid-career managers who work in struggling entrepreneurial firms find there is seldom a dull moment. In these chronically undercapitalized organizations, often dominated by a dramatic entrepreneurial personality, every day brings a new crisis. Like England's colorful monarch, Henry VIII, the entrepreneur is often a dashing and erratic figure. He typically rushes about and ignores organizational levels in his zeal to put out today's fires in finance, sales, or production. He is inclined to shoot from the hip on the basis of his own partially analyzed decisions.

The withdrawn, austere, remote—almost godlike—figure is another type who often founds an entrepreneurial organization. He spurns interaction with all but a few trusted subordinates. Occasionally he emerges from his castle to deliver pronouncements or to criticize the efforts of underlings. He may remain visible long enough to give a few lofty and sometimes confusing orders. Then he disappears into his retreat once more.

Mid-Career Problems in an Entrepreneurial Firm

Strong subordinates are likely to threaten the entrepreneur's need to exercise unilateral power and control. This type of manager usually leaves the organization after a difference of opinion with the owner over policy. More compliant subordinates find themselves picking up last-minute tasks that the entrepreneur drops as his mood shifts or as his personal overcommitments bog him down. Willingness to grab the ball and run with it in whatever direction the entrepreneur asks is important for survival in such firms.

When subordinate managers in the entrepreneurial firm reach mid-career, the unpredictable gyrations, stresses, and uncertainties associated with their work become less enjoyable. Many come to realize that the boss is a chronic promoter who will promise anything to anybody in order to get out of an immediate crisis. If the great man eventually does make good on his promises to share, he lets his subordinates know that these beneficences are bestowed as a personal favor.

After spending many years in this type of organization, the mid-career manager is less inclined to get charged up when the boss calls at midnight and tells him to catch the 8:00 A.M. flight to Denver or wherever. The manager comes to learn that such quick trips are usually generated for the purpose of "working on that hot new deal that has just come up—and I expect us all to pitch in to get the order." Actually, the entrepreneur may simply want an expenses-paid visit to his daughter who lives in Denver so that he can see his grandchildren. He uses the "current crisis" and "great opportunity just around the corner" techniques to whip up subordinates' enthusiasms.

Variations on the "do or die for good old Company X" ploy involve working long nights and weekends because the frenetic owner has once again made impossible delivery promises to sell a new customer. Like the 8:00 A.M. trip to Denver, such round-the-clock races to get the order out become less enchanting to subordinate managers as they reach mid-career.

For some individuals, however, a life of dedicated service in this type of organization has considerable psychological rewards. At retirement, these loyal managers who have given generously of themselves in the entrepreneur's service can look fondly back on the good old days. They enjoy reminiscing with deep feelings about "how we old-timers helped J.B. build the business." It is necessary for the entrepreneur to surround himself entirely with managers who are cast in this mold of personal dedication if he is to avoid dissatisfaction and high turnover among subordinate managers.

WORK LIFE IN THE ACQUIRED OR MERGED ORGANIZATION

During the past ten years, the number of mergers and acquisitions among business organizations has increased rapidly. This is part of a trend toward growth through purchase rather than growth by expansion. The mid-career manager in the acquired or merged organization usually encounters some personal adjustment problems in fitting into the new situation. The acquiring organization's philosophy, methods, and practices are usually different from those of the company he works in. Changing to fit into the new framework requires both perceptiveness and personal flexibility.

Sometimes the dominant organization immediately installs sweeping changes. New systems and methods are brought in rapidly. In other takeover strategies, the acquired company is allowed to operate in its old ways so long as profits are acceptable. In nearly all cases, new financial controls and planning systems are imposed by the acquiring firm fairly early in the game.

Mid-career managerial adjustments in an acquired company center around differences in expected managerial behavior between the old and new organizations. In the former, the manager had come to know pretty much where he stood. He had a recognized status, a seat in the managerial dining room, a certain size office, and predictable work assignments.

In some takeover situations the organizational transition is hectic and upsetting. Old ways of planning, coordinating, or measuring results are either devalued as ineffective or thrown out completely. The acquiring organization often sends its bright consultant types down from headquarters, who tell the mid-career manager what changes he will have to make to hold his job in the new order of things.

Where the home-office consultants are tactful, pleasant, and cooperative, the transition is less emotionally difficult for the manager, who has a number of years invested in older ways of operating. Unfortunately, the corporate consultant from headquarters sometimes is perceived as domineering, aggressive, and unreasonably demanding. The corporate man is often younger than the mid-career manager, an age difference that can increase the older man's sense of strain in the new situation.

If the young, usually technically trained corporate consultant is in a hurry to make a name for himself at headquarters, he is inclined to throw his weight around in the acquired company. Consciously or unconsciously, such men devalue members of the acquired company's management group.

The mid-career manager has a limited number of choices if

he finds himself in this type of acquisition transition. He can do what the new organization wants and make the acquired adjustments. Or if he does not believe in the new way of operating, he can rebel and probably wind up resigning—even at the expense of some of his stock option or retirement benefits. Depending upon his individual career prospects, the size of his mortgage and bank loans, and his skills in getting another job if the country is in a period of economic downturn, the manager may only have the first option—adjusting to the new situation as best he can.

What can happen in such situations is considered from two points of view: that of Jim, a hard-hitting young consultant, and that of Ken, an executive vice-president in an electronics firm that was acquired by a larger organization.

The Company Consultant Sent In to Turn an Acquired Company Around Fast

Jim, an internal consultant, was sent in by the president of an acquiring company (company X) to effect quick short-range profit improvements in a small acquisition (company Y). Jim had previously worked for five years as an external consultant to company X, whose president then hired Jim as an internal consultant on a two-year contract basis. The general understanding was that Jim would get a key vice-president's job in corporate headquarters after he had been on the payroll for a year or so.

Jim's first internal consulting assignment was to go to company Y, whose headquarters and two plants were located in a medium-sized city in the Southeast. Jim's new boss had negotiated only a vague agreement with the president of company Y regarding Jim's role on this assignment. Both company presidents agreed Jim should "look around and make recommendations as quickly as possible for improving profits and operations." Nothing specific was said about how Jim should bring this about, and Jim's authority to act was left a gray area.

Jim analyzed the operation as he would if he were still functioning as an external consultant. He decided that both the vice-president of marketing and the vice-president of manufacturing in company Y were not capable of doing their jobs. Indirectly he let both men know how he felt. He further suggested to the president of company Y that these men would have to be replaced.

The president and his two long-time assistants felt Jim was wrong in his analysis. Threatened, the three men did their best to discredit Jim and his work. They implied Jim was "throwing his weight around" on the basis of incomplete information.

Members of Jim's management seminar pointed out to him that he had been dangerously insensitive in the way he had handled his first internal consulting assignment. They said that in their opinion, while he *might* be able to get away with this type of tactic as an external consultant, he was asking for trouble by employing it in an internal consulting role.

Jim's high-dominance style of interacting with people in subordinate organizations coupled with his blunt diagnosis of organizational problems created difficulties for him. The three executives in the company he was sent in to assist felt he was putting them on the spot. The corporate president who hired Jim now has to smooth the situation over or get rid of Jim.

Jim's mid-career problem stems from his having made two basic errors. First, he failed to get an explicit agreement between the two company presidents on precisely what type of objectives he was expected to obtain within what time frame. Second, he was too insensitive to realize that his hard-hitting style would probably bring hostility, resentment, and counterattack from the executives in the subordinate organization when he put pressure on them.

Jim did gain considerable insight in a management seminar about his impact on others. The question for Jim is whether he can modify his basic style enough to become more successful as an internal consultant. If he is unable to do this, he should go back to being an external consultant.

THE EX-VICE-PRESIDENT WHOSE JOB WAS ABOLISHED

Ken is a mid-career manager who was on the opposite side of the acquisitions fence from Jim. Ken was executive vice-president of a small but successful high-technology firm that was acquired by a larger firm operating at a lower level of technology. The acquiring firm, however, was run by entrepreneurs who were moving their organization in the direction of professional management.

Ken, with an electrical-engineering degree, had functioned well for three years as the executive vice-president of the acquired firm. This company depended heavily on Vietnam war contracts for its existence. As government contracts slacked off at the end of the war, key stockholders in Ken's organization sold their interest to the larger firm.

Although Ken had heard about the merger, it affected his personal job situation as though he had been hit in the face with a bucket of cold water. His old boss, the president of the acquired organization, called him in and said: "Ken, your job as executive vice-president has just been abolished. I'm giving you twenty-four hours to come up with a new job description."

Although he is relatively unemotional, Ken became so hostile about the *manner* in which his boss broke the news that he had to restrain himself from striking out. To work out his negative feelings, he took the day off and went sailing in his boat.

Ken finally decided to talk to the president of the acquiring company at the new corporate headquarters before writing up his job description. His immediate boss agreed and set up a meeting the following week between Ken and the corporate president. Unfortunately, communications fell apart in the scheduling of this meeting. When Ken arrived at corporate headquarters, the president was out of the country on a trip. After two days Ken did finally get to talk to him. This delay further heightened Ken's resentment.

Ken wound up with an important new job in his old organization as senior vice-president, but he was extremely upset at the way his job shift was handled in the merger. Consequently, he gave up his stock and retirement benefits and took the first offer made to him by an executive recruiter to become president of another company. A more sensitive handling of Ken, as a person, in this merger situation would have saved a valuable executive for both the acquired and the acquiring companies.

SELECTED READINGS

Robert Blake et al., *Corporate Darwinism* (Houston, Tex.: Gulf Publishing Co., 1971).

David Halberstam, *The Best and the Brightest* (New York: Fawcett Crest, 1972).

Eugene Jennings, *The Mobile Manager* (University of Michigan, Bureau of Industrial Relations, 1969).

Alfred Marrow, *The Failure of Success* (New York: AMACOM, 1972).

Orvis Collins and David Moore, *The Enterprising Man* (Bureau of Industrial Relations, Michigan State University, 1964).

Eric Berne, *Games People Play* (New York: Grove Press, 1964).

4/The Fast-Growth Organization

HARD-CHARGING entrepreneurs usually head up the fast-growth organization. Such men are usually personally dedicated to expanding and advancing the firm at the fastest possible rate. Their personal drive is often combined with the techniques of modern management. When this happens, planning, marketing, and financial programs are brought in to help maintain continuous growth.

WORK LIFE IN THE FAST-GROWTH ORGANIZATION

Work life is particularly zestful for managers in fast-growth organizations. Mountains are moved daily. Insurmountable obstacles seem to have been moved every time the company house organ publishes another issue. Job opportunities and promotions often come along beyond one's wildest early dreams. Increased authority, enhanced organizational status, even becoming an instant millionaire through stock options are the rewards enjoyed by many mid-career managers.

The heady exhilaration that comes with being part of a dynamic advancing organization is the most pervasive feature of life in a fast-growth operation. Progress, action, advancement all become commonplace during the *expansion phase*.

Expansion Phases

During periods of extremely rapid growth, reorganizations occur once or more each year. Promotions abound. People are physically moved from one office to another. New wings are hastily added to corporate and regional headquarters. Everything the company tries out seems to work spectacularly. Promotion-from-within policies insure important advances for nearly all managers. During the expansion phase, new job challenges, hectic travel schedules, unbelievably long hours, and heavy energy drains are regarded as very worthwhile. At times the rapidly advanced manager may have to pinch himself to make sure he is not dreaming about his career fortunes.

Leveling-off Phases

Most fast-growth organizations get hit with leveling-off plateaus at periodic intervals. Things return to a more even keel. Consolidations take place. Often red tape and elaborate new systems proliferate as headquarters attempts to tighten its control over field operations. Staff jobs multiply rapidly in preparation for the next expansion.

If the organization runs out of promotable managers, men from other companies are brought in to staff the next growth move. When this happens, intergroup tug-of-war situations often develop between the corporate old hands and the new group of outsiders. Old hands, who labored long and hard to build the company, are concerned lest the outsiders, who are usually better trained and often have more managerial experience, take over. In many fast-growth firms these internal struggles become quite heated. Feuding between the new experts and the conscientious old loyalists can absorb a good deal of the company's managerial efforts.

When the next expansionist phase comes along, both the old managerial group and the newcomers are so busy with growth problems that they tend to bury the hatchet. There is more than enough glory and reward for all members of management who are considered promotable.

Declining Phases

Many growth firms go through a series of expand, level off, decline cycles. A company usually declines because top management lacks the breadth of skill to manage a large organization. Fluctuations between increasingly brief expansion, more leveling off, and finally a series of prolonged declining phases are typical of many inadequately managed fast-growth organizations. With prolonged leveling off and decline comes increased competition among members of management for the reduced number of key jobs.

SPECIAL PROBLEMS FOR THE MID-CAREER MANAGER

Three major problems confront the mid-career manager in the fast-growth organization: the possibilities of burnout, overpromotion, and being bypassed.

Burnout

Managers in these organizations often operate under such heavy physiological and psychological pressures in getting their jobs done that they become physically or emotionally drained. These various types of exhaustion may be diagnosed as having a physical basis. "Mononucleosis" is frequently mentioned in these situations. Often the deeper underlying cause is bone-weary personal fatigue, a type experienced by front-line combat troops who have been subjected to enemy attack over too long a period.

Some top managers in fast-growth companies seem to be endowed with almost limitless energy and physical stamina. Perhaps this is one reason they join such organizations. They also frequently place a high value on physical fitness in terms of participating actively in competitive sports. Some play as hard as they work, hitting the entertainment spots at night after having completed a grueling day's work.

Top men so endowed with a strong physique and youthful energy reserves find it hard to understand why their less robust managerial associates become physically burned out. They are inclined to consider such situations as being caused by "tough luck." They may also privately feel that a certain percentage of managerial casualties may be the inevitable outcome of fast-growth challenges and advancement opportunities.

LARRY: A CASE OF BURNOUT

In his early mid-career, Larry worked as a highly competent technical specialist in a professional firm that serviced a number of top-level organizations. The board chairman of one fast-growth company was impressed by Larry's penetrating mind and his ability to handle the firm's technical problems. He brought Larry in as corporate officer in charge of his particular specialty.

After three years as a specialist, Larry wanted to move up in either line or staff management. Though he had had no significant experience or training in supervising, leading, or managing, the board chairman and the company president were happy to give him a chance. The extreme management manpower needs of their organization caused them to gamble on Larry's overall capabilities.

Top management put him in charge of three administrative units in headquarters. At that time the company was also installing long-range planning and management-by-objectives systems. Within the first six months it became obvious to many at headquarters that Larry's personal managerial style and his lack of managerial skills were frustrating his three subordinate managers.

Shortly afterward, Larry's peer, another administrative vice-president with little managerial training, was transferred into a new division. Acting again on a "corporate growth emergency" basis, the board chairman and president decided the best they could do was to put the other vice-president's three administrative units under Larry.

With this additional load, Larry's managerial shortcomings became more evident day by day. He attempted to compensate by putting in longer hours, and he tried to supervise his six subordinates very closely. He never did learn how to delegate effectively. The company's new management-by-objectives program was a shambles in his area.

Meticulous attention to detail had made Larry successful in his earlier work as a technical specialist. But this same approach as a top executive harassed his six subordinates. Overly anxious to please the board chairman and president, he began to send out confusing and conflicting orders and changed his subordinates' priorities without warning.

Larry's difficulties as a manager were complicated when the board chairman mentioned the company's need to move ahead more rapidly on promoting minority group members. For some unexplainable reason, Larry jumped into what he thought was an explicit assignment with both feet, giving orders and directives regarding minority group promotions. These directives crossed his own responsibility area and encroached on that of the vice-president of operations.

The prolonged physiological and psychological strain Larry had been under in attempting to manage his new job may have affected his judgment. His zooming ahead on an assignment he had never really been given brought about a difficult confrontation with the vice-president of operations. The latter properly faulted Larry for trying to exercise authority in another executive's area. The board chairman and president had no alternative but to support the vice-president of operations and censure Larry, telling him that he was an inadequate manager at his current assignment level. He was also told that he would have to improve rapidly to hold his administrative vice-president's job.

About this time, three of his six subordinates walked into the president's office—independently—and requested transfers. Each said that he had difficulty getting his job done with Larry as his boss.

These pressures affected Larry physically. He went into the hospital twice within a month with what the medical people diagnosed as mononucleosis. When he returned to work he experienced chronic fatigue and was also in sub-par health much of the time. As a result he became unable to administer the groups that reported to him.

The company medical director, after a discussion with the board chairman and president, insisted that Larry take a six-week rest and recuperation leave. When he returned, the two top men told him that he would either have to return to his original position as a corporate technical officer or leave. They pointed out that for his own health and for the company's continued growth, a manager with the necessary skills had to take over the administrative vice-presidential duties.

Management obviously erred in putting Larry in this growth situation in the first place. But there are several things Larry could have done to have avoided physical and emotional burnout. He could, and should, have:

- ☐ Analyzed the key requirements of his new job and done his best to acquire the necessary skills;
- ☐ Taken interpersonal skills training to more effectively lead and motivate his subordinates;
- ☐ Taken management-by-objectives skills training to use the new system more effectively;

☐ Hired one or more trained and experienced assistants to help him with his rapidly increased workload when the three additional administrative units were unexpectedly dumped in his lap.

Overpromotion

Being overpromoted is the second key problem that mid-career managers may encounter. To meet expansion needs, managers frequently get advanced far beyond their current skill level—sometimes even beyond their level of ability. Promoting all managers who seem to have even an outside chance of handling higher responsibility is an important philosophy in most fast-growth situations.

Overpromoted managers eventually reach a point where they lack the managerial skills necessary to do their jobs. They are not given enough time at any single level to acquire adequate experience and judgment before the next promotion is hurled at them. When such managers have competent and well-trained subordinates, they can often get by even though they themselves are undertrained. However, in very fast-growth situations, every manager is promoted so rapidly that competent subordinates are very hard to get and hold.

Such continuous rapid organizational growth eventually results in a blind-leading-the-blind situation. A majority if not nearly all of the management group is deficient in skills, training, and sometimes in inherent capacities to manage at the levels they have been assigned to. Over a period of time, profit and growth fall off due to generally inadequate management at all levels.

Mid-career managers have to be objective about their own abilities and skills if they want to avoid being overpromoted. Such objectivity is difficult because the individual's inner needs to advance impel him to take the proffered step up without his bothering to analyze whether he has the ability to handle the new job.

Continuous managerial skill training and self-development are needed to avoid overpromotion. A bright manager who takes the time to develop the requisite new skills as he goes along is much less likely to wind up overpromoted in mid-career than is his counterpart who gets no such training.

Following are case summaries of two managers who were confronted with an overpromotion problem in mid-career: Marvin, who did little or nothing to cope with the problem during his meteoric rise to a top job in his organization, and Ned, who did a careful job of self-analysis.

MARVIN: A CASE OF OVERPROMOTION

An effective technical man in an important staff-support area of a fast-growth company's operations, Marvin wanted to move out of services and into staff or line management. He was bright, but he had an unfortunate habit of needling his corporate superiors on problems when he felt their thinking was less sharp than his. He was also basically a loner rather than an organizational team player. In confrontations with fellow managers, his basic intelligence usually made him look good, even though he lacked higher management skills.

This particular fast-growth company had been founded by four friends and associates. It had an astronomical, almost unbelievable, growth curve in a relatively new industry. Along the way, three of the founders dropped out of active management, although they all remained as key stockholders. With top managerial ranks depleted by their leaving, the board chairman promoted to the presidency a sales and marketing manager who had recently joined the firm. This new president had a strong, articulate, forceful personal leadership style, but his managerial skills had never been seasoned by high-level corporate experience.

Marvin felt that he was actually as good as, or perhaps even better than, his newly appointed boss. Marv's younger-brother-to-older-brother type of competitive attitude in his relationships with the president was never much below the surface, although he did manage to conceal some of it.

Marv was promoted to administrative vice-president in charge of several units, including the one he used to manage. In his old job he had had a number of highly qualified assistants who took most of the operating workload off his shoulders. But in the new job he had men reporting to him whose technical specialties he knew little or nothing about. Marv's managerial approach led him to operate largely as a memo man and an arm-chair general. Instead of interacting with his new subordinates on a personal, one-to-one basis, Marv held many formal meetings with his staff. He would then issue a flood of action memos as a follow-up to meeting discussions.

Without being aware of it, he failed to exercise direct managerial leadership in his new job. He might have gotten to know his subordinates and their problems through personal contact. However, his austere, introvertive, slide-rule approach caused him to minimize individual contact with assistants.

While he did not handle his new responsibilities with great success, he was rescued from having to face up to this fact in a curious way. The company decided to open up a new operating division and needed a new manager to run it. The early phases of building the new division required some of the technical skills that Marv possessed. The board chairman therefore offered the position to Marv. Although he had some misgivings about this move, the chairman felt there was no one else in the organization any better equipped.

The new job required the skills of a fast-moving leader with a good grasp of general management techniques. Marvin's style soon showed a number of limitations. He continued his addiction to "memoitis." His field trips to new operating units were of the fast-dash variety. In an effort to look at many things in a short time, he would fly into a city, make a hasty inspection tour, leave several vague and sometimes conflicting verbal orders, and then dash hastily off to the next site.

Marv might have succeeded in this job if he and the president had had a closer rapport and also if the president could have given him better coaching, counseling, and guidance. Marv also needed subordinates in the new division who had more skills than those possessed by the men assigned to him. In addition, he himself needed to learn how to manage a large organization more effectively.

None of these things occurred. Eighteen months after he started the new job, he and the president had a performance appraisal confrontation in which the president expressed his extreme dissatisfaction with Marv's results. The president attempted to work out a plan with Marv that would immediately improve the new division's performance. But Marv, partly because of his feelings of intellectual superiority to the president and partly out of his strong peer-rivalry attitudes, challenged the president's evaluation. Marv made what he felt was a good intellectual argument as to why he was right and the president wrong.

Their exchange degenerated into a win-lose situation. The board chairman was called in. Marv had the choice of going back to his original job of technical specialist manager or of leaving. Marv still feels that he was right and the president was wrong. He could not accept the demotion to his old job. So in mid-career he moved to a competing company. In so doing, he gave up a substantial equity in the long-term growth of the company he left.

Marv's case is one type of overpromotion in a fast-growth company. Spurred on by his personal ambitions to rise and advanced because of the company's shortage of trained men, he made two upward moves he was unprepared to handle.

Chapter 10 discusses ways in which Marvin might have analyzed the key factors in his situation so as to have avoided his overpromotion difficulties. The chapter also looks at several mid-career action plan options Marv might have used to avoid the situation.

NED: A SUCCESSFUL SOLUTION TO THE OVERPROMOTION PROBLEM

At the age of 40, Ned was made general manager of a new, small, but highly profitable division of one of the country's largest firms in his industry. As a chemical engineer, he had already successfully operated the company's largest production plant, set up a beginning technical sales group in a foreign country, and handled a variety of short-term staff assignments creditably. Over the years, however, he had done little to formally develop his managerial skills.

He confided to a behavioral consultant who was doing organizational development work with the company that he was thinking of quitting and going elsewhere. Ned's dissatisfaction emanated from the fact that two corporate staff men had been given the titles of vice-president and general manager when they were appointed to division managership jobs at the same time he was. He interpreted this to mean that he was out of favor with top corporate decision makers. In his opinion the two newly appointed vice-presidents had not demonstrated nearly the overall competence he had shown.

The consultant suggested to Ned that perhaps part of his problem was that he lacked sufficient *executive bearing* and *personal image impact* in his contact with the top corporate executives. Ned agreed to explore the matter. He did several things, among them taking a speech course and going to a tailor to get some better-fitting clothes.

The consultant pointed out to Ned that many top executives carry around in their heads a general success-image pattern, which concerns the overall image that they feel all key managers in their company should project. Such a pattern is subjective; unfortunately, it often has little to do with the objective performance results a particular man turns in. But it is a painful fact of organizational life that in many companies such images can affect a manager's career positively or negatively.

After Ned had polished his appearance and improved his speech, the consultant asked him to do a career self-analysis to see in which managerial areas he might be deficient in terms of what his new job as divisional general manager called for. As a result of this *career skills self-analysis*, Ned decided to take a general management course. In particular, he wanted to improve his skills in finance and marketing, since he saw himself as technically deficient in these areas. Then Ned took a course in specialized marketing in his product area and special voice training because his job required a lot of speaking at medical meetings.

At the end of two years, the consultant asked Ned what managerial skills he felt most of the top executives in the company were deficient in. He unhesitatingly replied that the lack was in the area of long-range planning. It seems that the company had had the first operations research group in the industry. The promotion-oriented sales types at the top had thrown out the operations research planning group because they simply did not know how to use its outputs. As a result, his company lagged badly behind their industry competitors in the planning area.

Ned then took two courses in long-range planning. As a result of all his self-development activities, Ned looked, talked, and acted like a much different manager at the end of this two-year period. His newly acquired skills added to the high-level performance of his division inspired the president to bring him back into corporate headquarters as his administrative assistant. Ned has learned and grown in this new job. In addition, he has continued his planned self-development program on a systematic basis. As a result of these growth activities, he stands a good chance of being appointed the next company president.

Some mid-career readers may protest that they can't do the same thing Ned did because they do not have authority to send themselves to special managerial courses. Even when this is so, they can still do a great deal to improve their promotional prospects through intelligent self-study and self-development. A recent study of 2,000 top and middle managers by one of the authors (Professor Pearse) indicates that the majority of such managers feel their principal managerial skills were acquired through self-study and self-development.

Bypassing

The third key problem for the mid-career manager in the fast-growth company is how to avoid being bypassed, which can hit the individual in mid-career particularly hard. It usually means that his advancement opportunities have ended or nearly ended insofar as that organization is concerned. In cases where the individual's ambitions to rise go beyond the level he has attained, the bypassed manager suffers strong personal frustration.

Not uncommonly, fast-growth organizations overpromote in the sense of giving high-level titles to a cadre of hard-working but sometimes limited supervisors who joined the firm early. Such promotions are both a reward for loyalty and a title increase in lieu of salary increases. The company often cannot afford to advance salaries at this stage of its growth. New titles are then a relatively inexpensive way to buy additional motivation and effort.

Some organizations that have gone through several years of fast growth wind up with 20 or 30 assorted vice-presidents on their hands as a result of the "give them titles since we can't afford to give money" approach. Like the annual rings on a growing tree, such vice-presidents become a record of past stages of organizational evolution.

As the company becomes large and complex, top management has to use more sophisticated techniques and skills. Many of the early-appointed vice-presidents are found to have limited ability to operate within the new framework. A frequent solution to the problem is to realign organizational titles in terms of actual individual competencies and skills.

This is why many growth organizations wind up with two or three levels of vice-presidents. At the lowest level are the plain vice-presidents. At the next level up, the managers bear the added title of "divisional vice-president." At the top of the status heap are the lordly "corporate vice-presidents." Under this system, a man may really function as head employment manager yet bear the title of vice-president.

Another frequently adopted solution is to put all the lower vice-presidents on various task forces in addition to their regular job assignments. Using the Parkinson's Law concept that "available work will expand to fit available time," such managers are sometimes kept happily active attending meetings of six or seven overlapping committees. Meanwhile, the top-level corporate vice-presidents, executive vice-presidents, and the president actually run the company.

AVOIDING THE SPECIAL PROBLEMS

Chapters 9 and 10 will go into more detail on self-analysis for self-directed change in mid-career. Here, however, is a general summary of things the manager can do to avoid getting caught in these pitfalls.

Avoiding Burnout

The manager can do several things to avoid burnout. First, he can lead as balanced a life as possible and refuse to become a compulsive workaholic. He can develop insight into his own managerial style to see if it habitually includes compulsive dedication to the job at the expense of a more balanced life.

Second, he can become more "maze bright" about maximizing his own managerial effectiveness. In many cases, he will have to become less of a doer and more of a manager and delegator to handle higher-level managerial responsibilities. To become less of a doer he will also have to sharpen his skills in personal time management and in effective delegation.

Avoiding Overpromotion

Overpromotion is, for many, a psychologically difficult phenomenon to avoid. Our American achievement traditions impel most of us to seek an ever-expanding career horizon. The astute mid-career manager who sees himself being thrust into an overpromotion situation can do many things to minimize the problems that usually accompany such a move.

For example, he can carefully analyze the key elements of the prospective job. He can then look at how the *success requirements* for this job differ from those of jobs he has previously held. Finally, he can concentrate his efforts on adapting and adjusting his managerial style and his skills to handle the new assignment as effectively as possible.

As a rule, advancing managers have to spend more of their

time on the strategic aspects of planning in the new job as well as on organization building and in leading and motivating their immediate subordinates. Often they have to shift their basic role and become more of a manager and an executive. This means spending less time on the technical-specialist—doer aspects of their work.

If he sees serious gaps in his managerial education, the mid-career manager can do as Ned did and take immediate steps to supplement formal management training with self-study and self-development. He can also do his best to see that his *crucial subordinates*—the assistants whose performance is crucial to his own success—are as competent and well-trained as possible.

Avoiding Bypassing

To avoid being bypassed in the fast-growth organization, the mid-career manager has to do at least two things well. First, he should be able to turn in as respectable a job performance as possible in each new promotional assignment. This way, the performance numbers or measurements of results used by his particular organization to evaluate him will be favorable.

Second, he has to become sensitive to the *success-image patterns* that the top decision makers in his organization consider important. Unfortunately, performance results and positive image are not always identical. Many high-performance managers get bypassed because they have not learned to project an adequate success-image pattern to the key power figures who decide their career fates. Maze brightness involves not only turning in good technical economic results on the job; it also involves awareness of the socio-political environment of the company. In your organization, what type of managers get promoted, by whom, for doing what?

Task-oriented managers feel their track records should speak for them. Often these men are independent and spend little time deferring to higher authorities. Nor do they go out of their way to cultivate, in the political sense, numerous friendly interpersonal and group relationships with associates. Unfortunately, in many entrepreneurial and bureaucratically run organizations, performance achievements alone are usually not enough to get a man promoted. In the ideal professionally managed organization, there would be a close correspondence between results, competence, and advancement. Most managers today, however, do not work in professionally managed organizations. Therefore they have to be realistic and practical about what it takes to get promoted in their organizations.

5/Mid-Career
Work Relationships

THE KINDS of interpersonal relationships we have on the job are important to our satisfaction both at work and in our lives as a whole. A temperamental, high-priced dentist who uses his assistants as outlets for his own ego gratification and out of a desire to push others around obviously creates uncomfortable work relationships. And the board chairman who takes personal delight in castigating and demeaning his divisional presidents for inadequate performance does just as much damage. In work situations where interpersonal relationships are positive, supportive, and collaborative, we all feel better.

Of course, the nature of managerial work, with its emphasis on attaining objectives with and through people, makes a manager's relations with fellow workers a critical facet of his career. Studies indicate that many managers spend up to 80 percent of their daily work schedule in some form of communications and in reconciling conflicts.

Communications take different forms at different levels in the organization. A manager has to sell his superiors, reach joint agreements with his peers, and lead and motivate his subordinates. In many organizations the cry, "If only it weren't for people!" becomes the crux of the mid-career manager's concerns.

FORMAL ORGANIZATIONAL RELATIONSHIPS

As previously discussed, the organization's climate, including its strategies and philosophies for dealing with people, sets the overall tone within which individual relationships between manager and others develop. In the entrepreneurial organization, trying to please the entrepreneur and to adjust to his changing moods and directives becomes the ultimate name of the game.

In bureaucratic organizations it is important not to rock the boat, to align oneself with the appropriate manipulative clique, and, in the technology-oriented bureaucracy, to know how to use the technology.

FORMAL VERSUS INFORMAL ORGANIZATIONAL RELATIONSHIPS

Most complex organizations have formal statements of purpose and goals. They also have policies and procedures that spell out how, theoretically, employees *ought* to relate to each other in reaching organizational goals. On paper, then, sophisticated organizations have a well-thought-out rationale for individual behavior designed to produce solutions to problems and to bring about maximum teamwork and accomplishments. In the real world, however, the formal organizational structure is often overshadowed by informal relationships and the ways people act toward one another.

Professor Melville Dalton was one of the early behavioral scientists to point out what actually goes on in the informal-relationships side of organizational life. He found that individuals and groups, or cliques, were involved in "buying" and "selling" internal information. In many cases, individual career ambitions and intergroup rivalries caused much of the manager's time to be spent in offensive attacking or in defensive survival types of exchanges.

Along with its formal rules and policies, each organization also has a set of informal and usually unstated group norms and standards. These have a powerful influence on how individuals get rewarded or punished. The maze-bright manager is quick to pick up these informal signals. Since each group tends to have a somewhat special and unique set of unwritten norms and standards, finding out what these rules actually require becomes one of the crucial tasks of the manager who is newly hired or is transferred from one work group to another within an organization.

Who stands up when who comes into a room? Are the greetings between two managers formal and polite or informal and casual, indicating a degree of personal intimacy between the two? What kinds of small talk or banter are permitted in what interpersonal situations? In bureaucratic organizations that have a large number of *ritual meetings* in which no productive output is really expected or desired, do group members quietly play the organizational charade in staff meeting after staff meeting and then privately express their frustrations about lack of progress to a few intimates?

Particularly in seniority-oriented bureaucracies, where benevolent paternalism prevails, top men are deeply concerned that subordinate managers are polite and deferent. If interpersonal exchanges are too direct or too much results-oriented in such organizations, the "old hand" becomes inwardly uncomfortable.

INDIVIDUAL PERSONALITY DIFFERENCES

In addition to the informal, largely ritualized behaviors that are built into company interaction patterns, the individual manager's personality or managerial style has a strong influence on his on-job behavior. Some have a blunt, domineering, aggressive style. Others are smooth and manipulative. Still others are warm, friendly, and not particularly ambitious. Some, indeed, may even be overly relaxed, tend to procrastinate, and are obviously underproductive. In fact, some have reached the point where they can be said to have retired on the job. A few may be impulsive, disorganized, and confused. Yet their political clique connections or their technical specialization or both may keep them on the job and provide them not only with a paycheck but, in some cases, with advancement.

As Professor Pearse pointed out in a recent article, in the absence of an effective management-by-objectives program, "managerial hustling" is the chief way to get promoted in many organizations. The skillful managerial hustler knows that image manipulation, which favorably impresses key power figures, may get him more rewards than will concrete performance. Naturally, he doesn't waste any more time in productive effort than he must. He is too busy projecting the right images to the right people. To get his job done, then, the mid-career manager has to learn to interact successfully with a variety of different types. This requires at least a minimum of flexibility on his part. In dealing with the aggressive-articulate type, for example, he may have to hold eyeball-to-eyeball confrontations in order to establish a working relationship. With the seductive-charmer type he has to be aware of the latter's consummate skill in wheeling-dealing and, in general, promising without performing. When confronting an arrogant-expert type he has to discount the individual's tendency to be a technical bluffer who either oversells his product or implies that all but members of the intelligentsia like himself are dolts and fools.

UPWARD AUTHORITY RELATIONSHIPS

In some of his boss-upward relationships, the mid-career manager will, one hopes, be fortunate enough to be working for a results-oriented person who encourages him to make a maximum contribution to their joint organizational goals. If the "fit" between both men is positive, the interpersonal relationship is likely to be congenial and productive.

But if the mid-career manager finds himself working for someone who is domineering, egocentric, or manipulative, their relations are likely to be difficult. Misunderstandings and negative feelings tend to accumulate as a result of the boss giving unclear or deliberately ambiguous orders or shifting his policy positions so frequently that subordinates have a difficult time figuring out what he wants from them. Working for such a boss may reactivate some of the early-childhood uncertainties the mid-career manager may have developed if either or both of his own parents used similar tactics.

On the other hand, if the boss is an austere, remote, distant figure who seldom says anything to his subordinate other than to criticize some performance, the mid-career manager may have trouble sorting out his present feelings from old memories and concerns about his relationships with parents who treated him similarly when he was young.

The ability to accurately sort out present-day reality situations with different types of bosses from childhood memories and anxieties is important in improving relationships with bosses. The organizational power structure, which supports the superior's ability to reward or punish, makes this level of relationship inherently complicated.

Social-Political Skills and Successful Upward Relations

Some managers have a highly developed set of socio-political skills that enable them to deal easily with a variety of different types of bosses. Such social specialists are adept at modifying their own behavior so to dovetail most comfortably with a variety of managerial styles. Usually this type of manager is an extrovert and has worked at developing his social-relationship skills since childhood.

In contrast, some mid-career managers, usually introverts, are low in social sensitivity and are not skillful at sensing social cues in their work environment. As a consequence they often fail to pick up even fairly obvious general signals from associates and superiors regarding the others' feelings. If the introvertive mid-career manager is also aggressively confident about his own ability to lead, direct, and make decisions, he may have chronic conflicts with bosses.

The highly independent manager also has frequent boss problems. He is unlikely to show deference to authority figures of all types. He resents being closely supervised, and he chafes at the constraints of rigid rules and policies.

Developing Skills in Working with Authority Figures

If the mid-career manager has not developed effective interpersonal skills in handling authority relationships, doing this becomes crucial for success in the mid-career years. Learning when and how to positively and constructively confront the boss will pay important dividends for the manager's own future. Learning how to work positively with different types of bosses is very important in the advancement of his career. He usually needs his boss's goodwill and personal endorsement to get a promotion.

Two key managerial skills, then, are the ability to work effectively with a number of different types of bosses and the ability to analyze correctly the organizational climate in which you work.

The Subordinate Who Made a Partial Adjustment

Orville is the type of manager who made only a partially successful adjustment both to his boss's managerial style and to the organizational climate in which he worked. After seven years in a management program for company A in which he felt he was not making enough progress, Orville returned to graduate business school and got his M.B.A. degree. His first job after graduation was in the management development department of a large, high-technology company.

The division in which Orv worked had a few highly competent men with M.B.A.'s. The technology of this particular division, however, was such that it had attracted, as key line managers, mainly high school graduates or graduates of four-year technical or engineering colleges. Eventually it was dominated by them. In addition, the ethnic background of the key power figures was different from Orville's.

During his first two years on the job he made a successful adjustment to his first boss. Orv was, by nature, an aggressive and articulate man who preferred to work independently. Orv realized that his boss, a bureaucratic old hand, was uncomfortable with the relationship. After some discussion with an organizational consultant Orv modified his manner toward his boss. He was able to do this painlessly without faking it and also without distorting his basic nature. As a result, their interpersonal relationship improved, and the boss recommended Orv for a promotion.

Orv's second boss was a manipulatively skillful M.B.A. who was extremely maze bright about the social patterns in this particular division. He gave Orv a free hand to run with the ball. Orv responded by developing and installing an effective management-by-objectives and management development program, which helped the division's performance considerably.

In the 1969–1970 recession, Orv's second boss left to set up his own consulting firm. Orv then reported to an old-line manager. At the age of sixty-two, this man was rounding out his career with the division. He never really understood what it was that Orv's group did. He also did not want to innovate during his last three years of service. He was afraid that a possible program failure would reflect negatively on his long, though not particularly distinguished, service in the organization. Tension between Orv and his third boss grew to the point where Orv's work output declined. In addition, during this period there was less need for the management development services that his group provided. Orv was given a choice between reporting to a personnel manager with a strongly bureaucratic orientation or leaving under generous severance terms. Feeling that he simply could not function under this man, Orv left.

Orv's basic problem was that his own managerial style did not fit the informal role-behavior requirements of this organization. In a bureaucracy where not rocking the boat was an important unwritten rule, he persisted in aggressively pushing through new programs. What's more, he came across to his fellow managers as somewhat aggressive, though he did not intend to be. If he had worked hard at becoming a more persuasive communicator and a better internal salesman, Orv probably would have been more effective in installing the programs that his creativity generated. Partly because his personal style did not fit the company pattern, he left.

LATERAL RELATIONSHIPS WITH PEERS

Good peer relationships in organizational life are complicated by many factors. Formal organizational structures often leave important *interface areas* between work units undefined. The amount of intergroup teamwork required to get the job done is not spelled out. Rather it is left to department heads to negotiate jointly. As a result, interpersonal and intergroup conflict and competition are frequently found.

In addition, organizational promotion and pay systems are often constructed so that each department head is rewarded in terms of his own group's performance, even though collaboration between two or more groups is required to get work out. These two forces basically make peer cooperation and collaboration difficult. Along with these factors, peers may be in competition with one another for available promotional opportunities. In such situations, if one managerial peer does extend full cooperation to another, he could wind up cutting his own throat by helping his peer look so good that the latter gets the promotion.

Strong patterns of peer relationship rivalry are often generated in family living during childhood and adolescence. The typical American family, with its emphasis on individualism and rewards for achievements in the classroom or on the athletic field, does little to encourage and train brothers and sisters to develop positive relationships with one another. When such family attitudes are carried over into organizational life, teamwork is further complicated. The *profit-center* concept, as a company reward unit, attempts to build *superordinate goals* into organizational life. In the well-managed profit center, individual managers cannot get a bonus unless the larger unit, the center itself, is profitable. As a result, peers must pull together if they want such rewards.

Both entrepreneurial and bureaucratic organizational climates often covertly encourage or condone peer negotiations that are characterized by bluffing, manipulating, short-changing, and outmaneuvering. Where such transactions are part of the informal organizational patterns, it is difficult or impossible to generate trust and teamwork. In many organizations, managers complain that "we just can't seem to get any teamwork going around here." Yet if a manager did offer complete trust and cooperation, he would be putting himself at the competitive disadvantage in the job-promotion race.

In mid-career, peer relationships often become particularly important for the manager, for they may be essential in building an informal network of mutual aid.

Some managers are more skillful at gaining peer support than are others. One type of manager who has difficulty in this area is the individual who had a great deal of competitive, aggressive hostility toward his brothers and sisters in childhood. Such attitudes often carry over into work relationships. Associates, sensing his desire to win out over them, withhold their cooperation whenever possible.

The introvertive loner has difficult peer relationships on the job. He has few friends or few informal contacts among his peers. Arriving at work in the morning, he interacts with fellow workers only as the situation requires. He leaves at the close of the day without having given or received very much from them personally.

Some loners are frequently unaware of their social inadequacy. Others are so involved in personal hobbies and interests that they see their jobs merely as a means of getting paychecks.

Still others have all of their social needs served by friendships off the job. This type of manager feels little need to improve his peer contacts at work.

Many mid-career managers can benefit by analyzing the quantity and quality of their present peer relationships and seeing to what extent they are currently positive and helpful. Should they find that their present relationships are poor, they can take steps to improve them. Such steps require both improved communication and outgoingness and increased empathy for and interest in one's fellow managers.

A MOVE TO A SMALLER COMPANY

Paul is a mid-career manager who is currently involved in a win-lose conflict with one of his peers. Now 57, he spent the first 25 years of his managerial career as an engineer and plant manager in one of the country's largest corporations. Feeling his career opportunities were limited in that organization, Paul accepted an executive recruiter's offer to join a small but promising entrepreneurially run firm. His new job made him vice-president of operations.

In an effort to bolster the organization's marketing capabilities, the entrepreneur-owner also brought in, via the executive recruiter route, a well-trained marketing executive who had worked for another of the country's largest corporations known for its aggressive and successful marketing programs.

Two years after Paul and his marketing peer joined the smaller company, they became embroiled in a win-lose conflict. Both managers are strongly competitive. Each has a keen enjoyment of outmaneuvering competitors. Since each desires to wind up in the No. 2 spot in the company—the executive vice-president's job, which is currently vacant —each is trying to outpoint the other.

In a training seminar, with his caustic humor and derogating one-upmanship style, Paul gave the other members of his group the impression that he was a "sniper"—one who likes to keep others off balance. At a key moment, a fellow group member stalked across the room and took a seat opposite Paul, saying he was sick of waiting for Paul to give people an opportunity to lead the group discussion. This rejection shook Paul up rather deeply at the time, but there is little evidence that this brief experience is likely to change Paul's basic style of interacting with peers on the job.

Meanwhile, there are indications that the entrepreneur-owner is becoming disenchanted with the interpersonal behavior of both Paul and his marketing peer. Sales are down. The constant intra-organizational bickering and gamesmanship the two men get into filters down to their functional groups. Organizational effort, which should be channeled into getting work done, is now spent largely in attack and defense between the two.

In some of these conflict situations, one or the other of the men wins out in the sense that the president appoints him to be executive vice-president. When this happens, however, the other man often leaves in a huff and his talents are lost. In other situations, the president goes outside and hires a strong executive vice-president to get both men to work as a team.

Regardless of the outcome of Paul's conflict, it is unlikely that the organization will win. Several years are often required to eliminate the negative byproducts of such a blood feud between two top men. Had Paul possessed more positive interpersonal skills, and had he not enjoyed the vendetta quite so much, very probably he could have earned the executive vice-presidency through promotion. Had he taken a different approach, there was also the very good possibility of his winning the personal support of his marketing colleague.

DOWNWARD AUTHORITY RELATIONSHIPS (SUPERVISION)

Behavioral scientists have paid a great deal of attention to managerial leadership and superior-subordinate relationships during the past 20 years. Many factors have contributed to the shift in supervisory practice that took place from 1950 to 1970. Perhaps most important is what Peter Drucker refers to as the rise of the "knowledge worker." As industry becomes more technologically sophisticated, more and more knowledge workers work in organizations.

Along with this phenomenon there have been vast changes in organizational life regarding the feelings and attitudes of three major segments: minority groups with their aspirations for advancement, women with their women's liberation claims, and young adults regarding jobs and supervisors. In many cases, these groups have forced a change in the nature of managerial leadership.

Evolution of Supervisory Philosophy and Practice

There has been a marked evolutionary trend in accepted supervisory philosophies and practices. Although each of the three types of supervisory styles described below is still practiced, the long-term trend has been away from the first two toward the latter.

The first type is often labeled the *tell* style. This is the old ball-bat, rock-'em-sock-'em style of the authoritarian, high-dominance manager. In the tell approach, the superior simply indicates to his subordinate what he wants done. Little freedom is delegated to the subordinate to use creativity or personal initiative. Delegation of authority is minimal; it is limited to doing what the boss wants done with no questions asked.

There is still a good deal of the tell style of supervision in low-technology operations or assembly-line situations. This style creates a minimal desire on the part of the subordinate to make much of a personal contribution to the work effort. He draws his paycheck while resenting the psychological pushing around his boss gives him. Many organizations dominated by the tell approach to leadership wind up with strong unions, which act as countervailing forces to offset management's dominance.

The second type of supervision can be described as the "*tell and sell*" kind. This kind of boss enjoys manipulating his subordinates. He has his own ideas about what he wants them to do. In deference to today's democratic philosophy, he plays manipulative games with his men rather than giving them direct orders. Usually well equipped, with a hard-sell style, the "tell and sell" boss attempts to maneuver his men into doing what he wants. This gives them the illusion of having freedom and initiative while he pulls the strings behind the scenes.

Subordinates quickly catch on to the "tell and sell" type of manipulations. They work to protect themselves against being had through his ploys and stratagems. This type of supervisory-subordinate relationship winds up like a chess game; each individual tries to outplay or outsmart the other. The result is the pattern of interpersonal maneuvers that Dr. A. H. Chapman, the noted psychiatrist, has written about. Instead of doing much work, boss and subordinate spend much of their time in maneuver and countermaneuver.

The third type of supervision—the type that seems to be most appropriate to our increasingly high-technology knowledge-worker society—has been referred to as the *joint-problem-solving* type. Organizations that encourage joint problem solving as a boss-subordinate relationship style are usually involved in management by objectives, long-range planning, and human resources activities. These are people-building rather than people-using types of organizations. Their intent is to create conditions in which subordinates are motivated to contribute through job challenge, recognition, and opportunity to take initiative. Monetary rewards are related to actual objectives attained.

Changing Managerial Style in Mid-Career

Some mid-career managers learned their styles of behavior under bosses of the old "tell" school. The pendulum began to swing away from this style with the human relations movement in industry that began in the 1930s and 1940s. It continued to swing further as more and more knowledge workers entered industry.

For a manager who copied the old pattern during his early years and who works in an organization that is beginning to shift in the direction of management by objectives, adopting required new behaviors can be irritating. Marked shifts in our habitual behavior patterns usually require some psychological readjustment since they are deeply ingrained.

Larry Revisited: An Example of the "Tell" Style of Supervision

Larry, the manager in the fast-growth organization with a burn-out problem, can attribute some of his stresses to limited supervisory abilities. When he moved into the administrative vice-president's job, he got no supervisory skill training.

The problem was more the company's fault than Larry's. The board chairman and the president knew that Larry came from a highly specialized technical background. They also knew when they transferred him from corporate technical specialist to administrative vice-president that he had had little or no training in managerial leadership. They hoped, as do many key decision makers in fast-growth organizations who are desperate to fill managerial gaps, that he would somehow "pick that sort of thing up as he goes along." Unfortunately, Larry never did.

Every Monday morning he called each subordinate in for a one-to-one review of the past week's performance against objectives. Larry himself was anxious to please the board chairman and the president in the most minute detail. He became uneasy when a subordinate indicated, in review sessions, that he had given a lower priority to one of the president's minor projects than to a project that stood to make a significant contribution to the company's continued growth and profit. Larry might be considered unreasonably eager to please and placate the men above him. He worried if he did not tightly control all details of the projects he delegated to subordinates.

As a result of Larry's supervisory style, each of his three quite talented subordinates complained to the president. They were willing to risk losing their jobs to express discomfort about this type of supervisory leadership. Since the company had a sincere program of human resources utilization, the president made it one of his own key assignments to help Larry improve. Instead of reprimanding the subordinates for going over Larry's head, the president diagnosed the subordinates' protests as a sign of low motivation and morale stemming from Larry's lack of training.

Then Larry was hospitalized because of physical illness. When he returned, he was moved back into his old job as a corporate technical specialist for health reasons. Top management solved the problem by transferring Larry, being uncertain of his ability to function better as a supervisor even if he were given training.

Interpersonal Stress Sources

Several areas in relationships with subordinates may be stress-producing for the manager. Some of the reasons why they are lie within the mid-career manager himself. He is reaching an age when he realizes that he has difficulty competing with younger men in terms of energy and drive. Many of these younger subordinates may have more formal education and training than he. Some will have strong ambitions to rise rapidly. When a subordinate's personal ambition is coupled with an opportunist attitude, the superior is reluctant to trust him. He fears the latter will pull an end run and sell himself up the line. Either or both of the following factors may contribute to the mid-career manager's feelings of stress:

Competitive anxieties and hostilities. Particularly with the rise of the well-educated, affluent younger generation whose values often differ from those of the mid-career manager, he may feel insecure, jealous, or resentful. Should he be having difficulty in working out relationships with his own children, his irritation with his children may unconsciously increase the tension he feels in dealing with younger subordinates.

Displacement regrets over one's "lost youth." As Bill, the mid-career manager we discussed earlier, expresses it, "I'm not young anymore." A competitive college athlete who sought to maintain his physical competence in mid-life, he mentioned his feelings of hostility and resentment in athletic competition with his own 18-year-old son.

Many managers in mid-career today were born during the 1930–1940 depression and grew into early adolescence during World War II. For many of them, their early lives were marked by material shortages, job insecurity on the part of fathers and older brothers, and relative personal privation. It would not be unlikely for them to resent the freedom of younger subordinates in dress, morals, and life-styles.

Often those in mid-life today feel squeezed between the older and younger generations. They are required to support their older relatives and to show them a degree of formality, respect, and deference that is a carryover from the era in which they grew up. Yet their own children behave in a manner that they might see as lazy, indifferent, shortsighted, and self-centered. The mid-lifer who behaved that way in his own early years probably would have been thrown out to make his own living. Yet this same man as a father feels obligated to support his own son should the latter decide to be a dropout.

Perhaps it is understandable that today's mid-career manager feels uncomfortable in supervising younger subordinates who reject the work-ethic values that are often at the core of his own convictions of what makes a man worthwhile. Should this discomfort become mixed with resentment toward younger people in general "not carrying their fair share of the load," he may take his feelings in this area out on his subordinates.

Resentments might be particularly keen if the older man

feels he had to give up some of his own youth during the depression to start earning a living. When he deals with more casual young subordinates, his own early feelings of personal regret may intensify his inner frustrations.

THE MANAGER WHO HAD DIFFICULTIES WITH HIS CHILDREN

Ralph is a mid-career manager who has worked very hard since leaving high school some 25 years ago. He has risen to a responsible position in his organization through hard work. His wife has taught school for the past 12 years, and they have a fine home and a reasonable amount of savings.

Ralph speaks of his son this way: "When he was 18 he graduated from high school. He was a bright boy and could have gotten chemistry scholarships from three universities. But he was crazy to get married, and wanted to go to work right away. So he married this girl. I didn't think it would work out, but what can you tell young people these days?

"He is now 23 and in the process of getting a divorce. His wife just wanted out; she felt marriage was too confining and wants to live her own life. Now my son is living at home and is beginning to save some money. Fortunately, he won't get hit hard with alimony payments. We lent him money to buy a car—his former wife took theirs, plus all the furniture; he needs a car to get to work.

"A few weeks ago he came to me and said he was thinking about going to college. At this stage in his life he realizes the value of an education. So my wife and I will be glad to help him if he has really made up his mind and wants to study.

"I also have a daughter, who is 18 and will graduate this June. She wants to go to college because many of her friends are going, but she has no idea of what she wants to do in the way of a future career. I can't see spending $3,500 or more a year sending her to one of the larger schools. She is good in math and science. I told her she ought to go to our local community college for the first two years to see if she develops a clearer idea of what she wants to do. I am absolutely against spending a lot of money sending her to college unless she has a field she wants to study for.

"My wife and I came up the hard way. We worked and saved as much as we could. We want our children to have a college education and to get ahead in the world. We are willing to help finance them in this respect. But young people today don't seem to know exactly what they want to do; they don't have much personal motivation as we did when I first started to work. I notice this on the job, too. While you can motivate the younger ones to some extent by job challenge and job enlargement and things like that, which our company is now trying, most of my younger people simply don't see the point in knocking themselves out to work overtime on nights or Saturdays. In a way, I understand how they feel. But it does make the supervisor's job tougher when you can't count on that built-in desire to get ahead that many of my generation had."

A Supervisor's Generation-Gap Conflict

Sam, a refinery manager for one of the country's largest companies, says frankly: "I see a generation gap between the older guys who are now middle-aged, like myself, and some of the younger managers and supervisors we now have coming along. The young people have different values and attitudes.

"While many of us got married and started a family and got saddled with house payments and things like that, some of our younger managers simply lead a different life now. They are more interested in skiing, sailing, or traveling around the world. Some of them don't get married at an early age, so they don't have family financial responsibilities. In other cases, you see what people call the dual-career family, where both husband and wife work and have a good joint income.

"When you ask the younger manager today to work overtime to handle a crisis situation, he often does it with great reluctance because it interferes with his weekend or vacation plans. I'm not saying they don't have a perfect right to feel this way. But it simply makes it harder for those of us who are running the refinery to count on that over-and-above-the-call-of-duty attitude that was sort of ground into many of the depression generation.

"I remember one weekend when I was just starting out in refinery management. We had had an upset condition in the chemical products unit I was in charge of. We worked around the clock from Friday until Monday afternoon to minimize the losses. As it was, it cost the company about $50,000 and I was very concerned because it might have made me look bad as a young manager—even though the fault was an equipment failure.

"That Monday, a member of the corporation's board of directors was driving a foreign visitor around the refinery yard and saw the messy situation of dirt and spilled chemicals all over the unit. He stopped and asked me why the housekeeping was so bad. I remember my feelings as I told him we had been working for two days to save the company money. He complimented me and the crew and got in his Cadillac and drove away. Later I learned he had called the refinery manager and said good things about my 'motivation'—I guess that's the word you use for it these days."

SELECTED READINGS

Melville Dalton, *Men Who Manage* (New York: Wiley, 1959).

Robert Pearse, "The Fine Art of Managerial Hustling," *Personnel* (September-October, 1973).

Peter Drucker, *The Age of Discontinuity* (New York: Harper & Row, 1969).

A. H. Chapman, *Put Offs and Come Ons* (London: Cassell, 1968).

6/Personal Development in Mid-Career

THE 20-YEAR period between 1950 and 1970 saw the greatest overall career advancement opportunity in American business history. This unusual situation was due to several factors. One was a shortage of trained managers resulting from the depression and World War II when managerial training was limited. Another was the unprecedented growth of American business organizations, both domestically and overseas. In addition, the need for trained managers to administer increasingly complex organizations in a high-technology society became important.

Prior to the 1950s, it was traditional that a manager would work most of his life with only one or two companies. Career progress then depended primarily on opportunities that developed through growth of the organization in which he worked. Managers who changed companies more than two or three times in this era were considered job hoppers and therefore a risk. At the extreme, the job-hopper label connoted possibilities of personal instability, interpersonal difficulties, and possibly disloyalty and undependability.

In sharp contrast, the practice of moving from one organization to another in search of career opportunities has, during the past twenty years, become commonplace. Executive recruiters, referred to as "headhunters," now make intercompany career mobility respectable and relatively painless. Business magazines report that managers at all organizational levels move from one company to another with ease, changing for what they expect will be greater career opportunities and job satisfaction.

COMPANY MANAGEMENT-DEVELOPMENT PROGRAMS

To fill managerial vacancies caused by growth and expansion, many larger firms set up in-house management training and development programs. Such organizations customarily hired potential managers at the bachelor's-degree level. Then the company sent them through a series of planned on-the-job and off-the-job training sessions to prepare them for advancement.

The increasing interest in hiring Master of Business Administration graduates brought more and more managerial employees in at this level. Since this type of employee had received a significant degree of business training in school, he was often able to make an immediate contribution to the company's progress.

MANAGERIAL ADVANCEMENT AND FAMILY STABILITY

Today's mid-career manager is usually interested in both job security and advancement. His older brothers and father may not have had these advantages because of very limited organizational growth during the depression. Many mid-career managers place a great deal of emphasis on advancing. Increased organizational status and salary are important to them. The opportunity to get ahead means they can give their families some of the material benefits they themselves may have lacked in their own early years.

Climbing the company promotional ladder during the wide-open period from 1950 to 1970 frequently required geographical moves from city to city as transfer assignments came up. The company held out the carrot of increased salary plus responsibility advancement as a reward for its mobile managers. Many firms expected all managers they considered promotable to automatically be ready, eager, and willing to accept such transfers. Their willingness was considered a sign of personal commitment to the company. Those who were unwilling to make such moves were labeled "undermotivated." Further career advancement opportunities for them usually ended if they declined such promotions.

Family strains and stresses that resulted from moving frequently from city to city hit the manager's school-age children hardest. During the '50s-to-'70s period it was not unusual for a family to move two, three, or more times within half a dozen years. For the school-age children, this meant making new friends and new school adjustments in each new city with painful frequency. For the wife, such frequent moves could, depending upon her temperament and adaptability, be either a stimulating change or a series of painful readjustments.

The mid-career manager who looks back at his own career moves as he reads this book may well feel that he really had no choice in these transfers. For some men, it was the only way in which they could acquire the breadth of organizational experience they needed to handle a higher-level job. When managers review their career history, some find the trade-off between organizational advancement and family stress an extremely difficult thing to measure. Many find in retrospect that their career moves left them with a lateral rather than an upward mobile pattern.

A CASE OF LARGE-CORPORATION MOBILITY

Ted is a mid-career manager who felt he had to accept a geographical transfer to one of his company's international subsidiaries if he wanted to advance into a better job. Speaking of his own career situation, Ted says:

"When I was in my late thirties, there were three of us in the department with M.B.A. degrees. We had all worked for about ten years in the finance division of this large corporation. After you had been there that long and had moved up the promotional ladder a few steps, it was mandatory that you get some field experience in one or more subsidiary operations, preferably in an overseas subsidiary. A lot of our profit and growth comes from these areas.

"A very good spot opened up in our French subsidiary. However, I didn't get it. Acting out of pique, I took the next one that came along. I felt I had to get out of corporate headquarters or risk getting buried at my current job level. The job opening happened to be in South America.

"My wife and I had one child when we went down there. Overseas tours of duty in our company are usually for three or four years. We had decided not to have any more children during this assignment for a number of reasons, but more children came along. As you can imagine, that upset our plans a great deal.

"To be completely honest with you, with the strain of these additions to our family added to very high living costs, neither my wife nor I are happy about the transfer. I find that I don't get along particularly well with the natives. Our company has a policy of hiring predominantly nationals in each foreign office. Only a few employees are Americans. I understand the political reasons for this, but it is not easy to get nationals to operate the way subordinates do in the States. Many of them are not particularly motivated to advance. Some know that the company will almost have to promote them because they are natives, so they do as little work as possible.

"Aside from a few American and English families in this city, we don't have very many friends. I suppose that's because our life-style is different from most of the people in the company office. I am on reasonably good terms with my boss, who is a national. We go over to his place occasionally. Sometimes we weekend with an English couple at a nearby resort. But with young children to take care of, these weekends aren't very relaxing.

"Another problem for me is that I feel very keenly that I am being underutilized in my present job. Most of the financial reports that we send back to corporate headquarters are routine ones that an assistant accountant could easily do. They don't require much financial sophistication. I'm not growing intellectually or in terms of corporate skills. Yet there really isn't much choice but to stick it out until the tour of duty is over."

Ted's situation involves a dilemma frequently encountered in the career patterns of relatively top-level staff men in large corporate headquarters. The company feels a man needs broadening, preferably in overseas experience, before he can become eligible for a higher-level promotion at headquarters. Unfortunately for Ted, his style is that of the reserved introvert. This makes it hard for him to meet new people. He dresses in the ultraconservative manner that was popular when he started his career as a young executive. His total life-style implies that he strongly values intellectual precision and "correctness." He has difficulty letting his hair down and interacting with others on an informal, person-to-person basis.

It is difficult to say how much of Ted's style may complicate his career mobility both at corporate headquarters and in his present overseas assignment. He did not get the choice European overseas assignment he was hoping for; an indirect implication of this is that he might not have represented the company well there.

His present discontents and negative attitudes are unlikely to improve his performance on this tour of duty. If he returns to corporate headquarters tagged with the image that he "lacks flexibility and the capacity to adjust to field assignments," his future career could be limited. He might wind up at a level below that which his education and intellectual capacity would otherwise qualify him for.

A Man Caught in Two Mergers in One Year

Victor has a somewhat unusual mid-career history. Through circumstances beyond his control, his company merged twice with two other organizations in less than eighteen months. Vic tells his career-decision story this way:

"When I got out of college, I went with a small company because I have always liked the freedom that goes with smaller organizations. You have to wear many hats as a manager and get involved in a lot of things you could never get into in larger, more compartmentalized companies.

"Our little company unexpectedly was sold to a bigger company after I had been there about five years. We were just getting over the shock of this merger when the second company was, itself, acquired by one of the industry's giants. This firm had its corporate headquarters overseas. In about twelve months we went from being a very small company to being a relatively small part of a very big company.

"It took about another year for the dust to settle from the second merger. None of us knew what would happen next. Finally one day, my new boss called me in and told me that the big company was transferring me to an office in one of its midwestern operations.

"Even today, it is hard for me to describe the shock I felt when I got this directive. I was always concerned about job security. During the depression I had seen my father sitting around the house out of work and I never wanted this to happen to me. On the other hand, my wife and I are east coast people. We couldn't really bear to make a move to a small city in the midwest with no friends or relatives around.

"I asked for two weeks to think it over, which they gave me. My wife and I decided we would say no and take our chances. Surprisingly, as it might seem, the larger corporation then asked me to go overseas to their corporate headquarters to take a two-year training program in their methods. This kind of thing is unusual when you turn down a first offer like I did.

"My wife and I liked living in that European city pretty well. I learned a great deal about the business. But seeing the vast bureaucratic setup they had convinced me that I was not cut out to work in a large corporation. When we got back to America I worked for this company for two years to pay back their training investment. Then I took a job with my present organization, which is much smaller. I think I will always be happiest in a small organization."

PSYCHOLOGICAL COSTS OF CAREER MOBILITY

American society strongly encourages career and personal mobility among its citizens. Public education makes career mobility opportunities available to all who have the intellectual capacity to benefit from formal education. There probably has been a greater degree of career mobility opportunity in the past 75 years in America than in the history of any country in the world.

Our national traditions favor career mobility. The strong desire for personal and social advancement gets built into most of us. During the 1950s and 1960s, career mobility for business executives often required extensive geographical movement.

The individual manager's extensive personal preoccupation with work and with the career advancements that frequently follow a heavy commitment to work often reaches a point where it becomes all-consuming. Jules Archer likens this problem to that of the deep-sea diver who suffers from oxygen intoxication after having worked in deep water for too long a period:

> A similar intoxication with work often seizes business executives, keeping them submerged in the murky depths of the corporate world for periods so prolonged as to endanger their private lives.

Losing their sense of perspective, they come to regard the corporation as their true habitat, and their homes as vaguely recollected spawning grounds to be visited from time to time.

John Fendrock feels that it is possible for an executive to lead a much more balanced life than many now do. His formula involves carefully analyzing your time-energy use patterns. Properly done, this puts the manager in a position to balance out his needs, goals, interests, and career work requirements in an optimum way.

Unfortunately, up until the past 10 or 15 years, society encouraged the workaholic to continue his compulsive job-related activities to the exclusion of other facets of a balanced life. Such areas as family relations, hobbies and interests, and community and friendships were sacrificed for job success. This pattern is presently in flux. Many younger managers have shifted their personal-work-versus-rest-of-life balance dramatically.

Increasing numbers of mid-career managers also are taking a look at their own time-energy use patterns, asking themselves fundamental questions regarding what they want out of life. Two previous cases illustrate this process. Al, the mid-career manager who habitually worked overtime, is one example of a manager who made a significant mid-career change. Frank, who decided to delegate his strenuous troubleshooting job overload to his assistants, is another.

EFFECTS OF LEVELING-OFF OF MOBILITY

The pyramidal nature of organizational structures means that the number of top jobs automatically drops off sharply the higher one goes up the career ladder. But our American tradition, which holds that a worthwhile man should keep climbing, drives managers to seek upward mobility at nearly all costs.

Mid-career is a time when highly ambitious managers can run into inevitable organizational barriers that limit promotions. In some large organizations, bumping one's head against the top of one's "career ceiling" is cushioned by stock options, extra vacations, being sent to posh management seminars, and the like. It is hard to be totally dissatisfied with a situation where you have a significant title, work that others regard as prestigious, and a good salary to accompany your managerial position.

Yet in those cases where the mid-career manager has identified his personal sense of self-worth with rapid upward advancement, even career mobility slowdown may be personally threatening. Particularly for the fast-track executive—the man who is moving spectacularly up the ladder—a mid-career decline in advancement may cause deep personal feelings of frustration. Research studies indicate that salary and advancement for most managers have a distinctive leveling-off time. Writing about this problem in *The Wall Street Journal,* Paul Lancaster stated in the June 22, 1972, issue:

> Graduates of the Harvard Business School are a talented and ambitious bunch. But there comes a time, usually about 15 years after they enter business, when the earnings of most of them reach a plateau. Their incomes "do not increase significantly thereafter," says a survey published by the *Harvard Business Review.*

Since the leveling-off of career advancement is a fact of life for many, the mid-career manager needs to do some realistic self-appraisal if and when this happens to him.

CAREER SELF-ANALYSIS AND ADVANCEMENT

There are several resources the mid-career manager can use to take an honest and candid look at his personal career-mobility opportunities. Chapter 10 will outline one method for setting up an action plan for mid-career self-development. Three of these resources are listed here. The first is objective self-appraisal and self-analysis. In each of the brief case summaries discussed in this book, the mid-career manager can maximize his potential by taking an objective look at himself. For example, Irvin, the manager with the bureaucratic blahs, Marvin, the manager who got into an overpromotion situation, and Ted, the disgruntled finance manager who resents his current overseas assignment, can all benefit by taking an objective look at their present managerial styles and their current levels of managerial skills.

In addition, the mid-career manager can review the success-image patterns of the types of people who get promoted in his organization. Like Ned, the manager who solved his overpromotion problem through planned self-development, the reader can improve his own promotion chances by self-analysis and self-development.

Finally, the mid-career manager should be as maze bright as possible about his organization in terms of how people get promoted within its particular structure. Until management-by-objectives programs work even better than most of them now do, it will continue to be an unfortunate fact of organizational life that the best-producing managers do not always get promoted and rewarded.

CAREER AND EGO

Mid-career is often a time when the manager seriously compares his ambitions with his actual attainments, and any discrepancies that exist can become problems. Some of the problem areas the mid-career manager is apt to face are listed below. The manager's ability to analyze these problem areas as objectively as possible is often crucial to his further advancement.

Success. Achieving rapid career success does not automatically guarantee a manager's personal satisfaction—even though our society says that it ought to. Some people feel their rise was accidental. If this is true, then a negative turn of fate could bring their ambitions crashing down. Others feel deep inside that they do not really deserve their success. They may feel both guilty and unworthy about having advanced by having gotten the breaks.

Failure. Society has some general definitions regarding what constitutes both success and failure. To the business manager, experiencing success or failure is often a highly personal internal evaluation of self. Objective measures of job results are usually not clear-cut. Most performance appraisal techniques are imprecise at best. The feelings a particular boss has toward his subordinates does much to color his perceptions of the subordinate's relative worth. In all too many performance appraisals, boss and subordinate don't level with each other. Too often the boss sends out oblique signals that the subordinate has to interpret as best he can.

"Dehiring" is currently a popular process. Here the subordinate who is judged to be limited is either eased out or pushed aside rather than directly fired. The unfortunate subordinate may have an office, a title, and a salary yet not be given any meaningful work to do. He may also be left out of significant committee meetings. Eventually he gets the message that there really are no productive and meaningful tasks for him to perform.

Conflicting life goals. Preoccupation with career success, as Archer mentioned, often means the mid-career manager has neglected his wife, his children, his community relationships, and even his hobbies to advance on the job. Living this unbalanced life sometimes causes the mid-career manager to wind up with a number of deep regrets centering around important things he neglected or ignored in his career climb.

If he sees his children having problems in school or in developing a sense of identity and strong motivations to achieve, he may blame himself for not having spent more time with them. Many depression-born mid-career managers who are very concerned about giving their children the material things they themselves did not have were too busy working to be good fathers. In order to earn the money with which to buy things, they have not had the time or energy to spend in developing relationships with their children. All the child sees is a harried father who is always too busy or too tired to go fishing or help with a scout troop or attend Little League baseball games or school functions.

Overpromotion. The manager's ability to take an objective look at his capacities and skills when offered a significant promotion requires a great deal of self-discipline. Since advancement is considered "good" in itself and since the individual is seldom sure whether he can handle the more responsible job unless he gives it a try, he has a strong built-in urge to accept all promotional opportunities that come along.

Unfortunately, some managers have found (to their regret) when they moved up that either they lacked the skills required or they were unable to make a sufficient change in their managerial style to adequately handle the new job. In most growth companies, the career path trajectory tends to be either up or out. This pressure makes it hard to turn down a promotional offer, whether the individual feels he can handle it or not.

Today the mid-career manager often takes a much closer look at promotional situations in terms of total life satisfaction than did his counterpart of 10 or 15 years ago. The latter almost always automatically jumped at a promotional opportunity because he felt there was virtually no alternative.

THE MANAGER WHO TURNED DOWN A PROMOTION

Walt, a 53-year-old manager, turned down a significant promotional opportunity. Here is the way he looked at it:

"Last year the company wanted me to leave California and come east to corporate headquarters at a top vice-president level. The home-office job would have paid more. But at my age, with our children grown and gone, my wife and I decided it wasn't right for us.

"We have lived in California for the past 15 years. The branch I am in charge of does very well. We have a very happy work crew. People like their jobs. I give them a lot of freedom to do their thing and they respond positively. I have taken up a hobby of rock gardening.

"My wife and I travel throughout the state searching out different rock gardens. In addition, the vacant corner lot, which I own, has been turned into a play spot for neighborhood kids. I am president of the neighborhood homeowner's association, and we have made many fine improvements in the section of the suburban community we live in.

"Looking at the company's promotional offer in this perspective, and taking into account the additional income-tax bite, I couldn't see giving up what we have here to go east and live in a condominium in a big-city suburb. I think the home-office people were disappointed at my decision. They even made me a second offer that involved more money. But I am very happy that I decided this way. I may not get promoted any higher, but my total life satisfaction is greater where I am now."

TILTING AT WINDMILLS

Some mid-career managers have ego difficulties in accepting the fact that younger, highly trained and technically oriented managers may be promoted over them. In the older, strictly seniority-oriented bureaucracies, this was seldom done. Those who came into the organization at the same time tended to be promoted at the same rate.

With the rapid rise of the engineering- and business-school-trained younger managers in the late 1950s and 1960s, this pattern has been upset. If the mid-career manager lets personal disappointments interfere with his work or with his work relationships with such rapidly advancing younger men, he may complicate his career situation needlessly. Handling personal disappointments is never easy. Managing career disappointments is especially difficult because of the social assumption that all men should advance continually.

The inability to sense major new organizational trends and to adjust to them is another form of windmill tilting that sometimes bothers mid-career managers. One major trend in the past years has been that technical marketing concepts are becoming the principal management approach. In former days, production schedules were the key factor in company planning. With the recent development of new products and increased competition for business, many old-line firms have turned to a more marketing-oriented approach to survive. Some managers who grew up in the older production tradition find it very difficult to adjust to the new organizational realities. Unless they can make the necessary transition, their careers suffer.

The Production Man Who Couldn't Adjust

Art is an old-line, production-oriented plant manager. Holding a master's degree in metallurgy, he runs a large metals plant in a high-technology end of the business. He looks about ten or fifteen years older than his chronological age. Tall and heavyset, he resembles the old "bull of the woods" type of plant manager who used to dominate production shops during the 1920s, '30s, and '40s. In discussing his mid-career situation in a management seminar, Art said to fellow group members:

"We have a lot of those young marketing-oriented engineers around our company. They come into my plant and try to tell me what to do in the way of adjusting production schedules to meet customer needs. They also want my plant engineers to take time from their regular work to give certain types of technical services to customers. Competition is getting tougher in our end of the specialized metals business. But how can I keep good production schedules with young squirts like that interfering? I simply tell them to go to hell and throw them out."

This training group, which had been working together on feeling exchanges for a week, included two young marketing-oriented engineers. Both men came from very large and modern corporations, though neither firm was in the specialized metals industry.

After Art had rambled on for 15 minutes about his resentment toward "marketing types," the two engineers began to get visibly upset. The blood rose in their necks and to their cheeks. Anger was beginning to show. Finally, one of them said:

"Art, I'm going to tell you this because I like you personally in spite of your hostile attitudes toward marketing-oriented engineers— of which I am one. Do you know what we do with old fossils like you in our organization? If they've been around for only a short time, we fire them. If they've been around long enough to be near retirement, we push them aside and give them a desk in some department where they won't get in the way of customer service or spoil our marketing plans. But either way, we get them out of the mainstream so they can't hurt our competitive position in the industry."

Art turned red. He felt angry and defensive for a few minutes after this strong confrontation with the younger manager. But later in the week he talked at length with both young engineers. They gave him more feedback about his situation, as they saw it.

Art later wrote the consultant who directed the seminar that this one incident had made a major difference in his career. He said that when he went back to the plant he saw that many of the things the two engineers said were happening in their organizations were also happening in his own company. Being intelligent, Art changed his approach to the engineering-marketing group. This self-directed change may well have meant the difference between his being bypassed or even put out to pasture until retirement and being recognized as qualified for later promotion to a job on the corporate manufacturing staff.

POSITIVE HANDLING OF CRUCIAL CAREER SITUATIONS

Some of the most crucial career situations involve overpromotion, too-rapid advancement, and being boxed in. Managers who are boxed in are usually so valuable in certain management jobs in organizations that lack a systematic management development program that they can never get free when a promotion comes along. "We can't spare you just now because everything is in an uproar. But I'll do my best to see that you'll get the next good opening that comes up," explains the boss.

Being miscast is another problem. The miscast manager has somehow gotten assigned to a job in which his primary skills and abilities can't be utilized. Consequently, he gets stuck at a level below that which he is capable of attaining in his field. The industrial engineer assigned to inspection on a temporary basis who five years later finds himself still supervising the inspection function is obviously miscast.

Effective handling of crucial career situations to prevent them from becoming crises can be accomplished relatively easily if the mid-career manager will take a few specific actions:

Adopt a career rather than a series-of-jobs perspective toward your work experience. By taking a career approach to prospective promotions, the manager can estimate whether or not any particular advancement opportunity is likely to result in a long-range improvement in his career situation. Some promotion opportunities wind up being merely lateral moves when viewed from a career perspective.

Phil, a mid-career manager, says this about his own career: "I'm the most laterally mobile manager in America today. I've 'lateralized' myself all over North America by holding six different jobs with three different companies." Looking back in mid-career, Phil realizes that if he had analyzed his past job-change opportunities more carefully, he could have avoided some of these moves, which in perspective were not actual advancements.

Make realistic adjustments to major organizational changes. Art, the old-line plant manager, had gotten farther out of step with company expectations with each passing year. Yet he made a necessary adjustment to the new engineering-marketing approach as the result of a fortunate incident in a management seminar. Had he not had this experience, he might well have suffered serious career difficulty by continuing to use his old approach.

Continue to grow and develop as a professional manager.
Marvin, the manager who was overpromoted to the vice-presidency of operations in a fast-growth company, did little or nothing to improve his managerial skills during the five-year period in which he received a series of very rapid promotions. He also did nothing about changing his managerial style on the way up. At lower operating levels, his outgoingness, his personal warmth, and his candor attracted a great degree of personal loyalty and job commitment from subordinates. But when he had to manage a large division through reports, phone conversations, and staff meetings, his personal touch was not enough. Marv simply never learned how to operate as a higher-level manager even though his job as vice-president of operations required that he do so. As a consequence, he chose to resign rather than be bypassed when the company brought in a new man from outside at his vice-presidential level.

SELECTED READINGS

Jules Archer, *The Executive Success* (New York: Grosset & Dunlap, 1970).

John Fendrock, *Goals in Conflict* (New York: AMACOM, 1968).

7/Mid-Career and Society

ANYONE WHO SAT in a gasoline line at 6:00 A.M. during the winter of 1974 does not have to be told that we live in a rapidly changing and often unpredictable world. Marshall McLuhan refers to our complex society, where advanced communications and transportation systems shrink vast geographical distances, as "life in the global village."

CHANGE IS THE NAME OF THE GAME

Instantaneous communication and rapid transportation make it impossible to escape the problems and pressures of the wider world and of world society. Between 1950 and 1970, the world underwent more technological and social changes than during any other period in human history. Prior to these changes, people lived more at a regional and local level. World news carried by newspapers and radio seemed relatively remote, of events happening somewhere else. Now the evening news brings television photos of civil wars, earthquakes, and plane crashes in living color. Confronted daily by the visual medium of TV, we can't escape personal involvement.

The Sunday edition of *The New York Times,* for example, carries careful analyses of such world problems as food shortages, overpopulation, inflation, energy and raw-materials shortages, and political revolts and their economic implications for our own standard of living and peace of mind.

In his opinion polls on changing social values, the social psychologist Daniel Yankelovich comments on the vast changes taking place in expectations, and on the feelings of "entitlement" (to a fair share of society's benefits) that minority groups, women, and young adults now have. This feeling of entitlement implies laying claim to a certain minimum standard of living by virtue of membership in American society. The old Protestant work ethic, which holds that individuals should work for what they get, no longer holds in the *entitlement era.*

FUTURE SHOCK

The recent vast number of technological and social changes we have experienced add up to what Alvin Toffler calls "future shock." All of us today, but particularly those in mid-career, are struggling to keep up with such major future-shock adjustment problems as

Overstimulation. Unlike previous generations, we are bombarded with an overload of messages and signals from advertising, television, radio, newspapers, magazines, telephones, road signs, and spoken conversations. The human nervous system has a limit to the number of messages it can meaningfully process and store without undue stress.

Information overload. We need feedback from our environment to function, for man is a feedback-processing animal. Without feedback signals, we become disoriented. On the other hand, like a telephone switchboard during peak phone hours, we can become confused and unable to function well if too much information comes in at one time.

Decision stress. In simpler societies and quieter times, most of man's decisions were programmed; that is, in most situations, people could use a set of habitual responses and come out fairly well. In this complex world, what were formerly simple decisions have become complex choice-problem areas. The commuting hassle described later in this chapter gives some examples.

Psychological and sociological stresses. These three factors (overstimulation, information overload, and decision stress) add up to a potential for individual psychological and social stresses. Some of these stresses are primarily symbolic. (Will we lose social status on the job if we transfer into a new department, take a smaller office, and share a secretary with another manager?) But others are really complex economic and personal decisions. Should a successful small businessman sell his business at age 55 because the workload is getting heavy and buy a condominium in Florida? If he doesn't sell, the work strain may eventually cause physical problems. If he does sell, and inflation continues, can he get into some type of *second-career* activity in Florida to supplement the money he gets from selling his business?

MID-CAREER: A TIME OF NEW OPTIONS

Until recently, most people in mid-life had relatively few options in terms of life-styles, career choices, and job satisfaction alternatives. If you were a sober, respectable member of middle-class society, you pretty much stuck with your traditional roles. The reward for having followed expected patterns was social approbation.

A Man Who Developed a Second Career

Today's mid-career manager is often confronted with more options and decision choices than his counterpart in previous generations. Calvin is a man who made such a mid-life career change. At age 53, he resigned his job as a successful vice-president of a major corporation, cashed in his stock, borrowed some money, and bought a dude ranch.

Since he had been a regular guest at this ranch for many years, he knew its operation firsthand. But in making this decision he was taking a risk that he might not be able to succeed in this type of work.

His reasons for making the decision at that particular age were twofold: the property was available then, and he wanted to make this career shift while still young enough to have the drive and energy to build the business and make it an eventual retirement venture.

ACCEPTED ROLES VERSUS PERSONAL SATISFACTIONS

Throughout most of human history, most people played their expected social roles with whatever grace and style they could muster. The life roles of wife, husband, father, mother, worker, and manager were relatively stereotyped and limited in terms of permissible variations on the main theme. In an economy of scarcity, people were too busy working to provide food and shelter to have much time to think about life and what they personally hoped to get out of it.

The present, more affluent age is much more concerned with concepts like *total-life satisfaction* and personal relevance. Considerations concerning what one wants to get out of life and what sort of person he or she wants to be have become increasingly intrusive.

More and more of today's mid-career managers are asking questions like "What's it all about?" and "What am I getting out of this rat race?" With a world in flux and younger generations openly departing from the older stereotyped life-styles and expected roles, many mid-career individuals also are looking at their own life situations from the new point of view.

COMMUTING HASSLES AND THE CLUB CAR TO OBLIVION

Any manager who lives some distance from his plant or office and is confronted with increasing expressway traffic and limited parking facilities has a daily struggle with commuting hassles. Those who suffer massive inconvenience from riding inefficient, dirty, and late commuter trains have a slightly different problem. One hopes that no single commuter will ever be exposed at one time to the problems described below. And yet, many commuters experience may of these problems each day they ride a train to work.

Our commuting hero drives like mad to catch the 7:15 (out

of New Canaan, Winnetka, or wherever). The village police in his suburb have set up one of their favorite speed traps. Fortunately, he is saved from getting a ticket by a crusading woman just returning from the station who, like Paul Revere, drives around blinking her lights to warn late commuters that the police are at it again.

He slows down to avoid the speed trap, so it is after 7:15 by the time he jams his car into the overcrowded suburban parking lot. As he runs puffing to the station platform, wondering if he will get a heart attack, he learns that the 7:15 is late again and won't be in until 7:42. That means that it will be overcrowded because other late-arriving commuters will also push and shove to get on board.

When his train reaches the outskirts of the large metropolis where he works, it makes its first stop at a station overlooking one of the city's worst slum areas. Looking down at the street, he sees squalor and thinks of the possible knifings, dope pushers, and all the other traumas of the urban slum. He wonders idly how many of the thousands of dollars he paid last year in federal income taxes are being used in this year's new slum rehabilitation project—and what, if anything, he is getting for this tax burden.

This thought brings up, in turn, a consideration of politics and politicians who direct the spending of his tax payments. Having lived through the New Deal, the Fair Deal, the Square Deal, the New Frontier, and the Great Society, he does not expect much in the way of permanent improvements from this year's tax expenditures for urban renewal.

Arriving at the central city train station, he climbs dirty stairs, walks in dirty, crowded streets, and finally arrives at his office huffing and puffing, 20 minutes late. His day is filled with meetings, memos, and phone conversations. Two small crises and one large one develop before lunch. He bolts a hasty lunch, with a business conference included, and then it's back to his desk. In the afternoon he learns that two organizational programs are being shifted—priorities have been changed again—and he gets involved in the reassignment of work to his own subordinates that these changes require.

Around 4:30 or 5:00 P.M. (or later, depending upon how

many last-minute things come up), he leaves the office to fight again for a seat on the homeward-bound suburban train. Considering the stresses of the day, it is little wonder that our mid-career manager often feels that the club car, with its beverages, is one of the few refuges left from a dismal outside world.

Should he manage to get both a seat and a drink, he considers himself fortunate indeed. As he opens the evening paper he is confronted by news of the latest international skirmishes, national graft scandals in high offices, urban murders and muggings, and a few gang wars.

Looking out the dirty train window, he may well think to himself: "Is this the club car to oblivion that people kid about at cocktails?" Reflecting on his job efforts and life in the suburbs, he may visualize himself walking a treadmill that never ends. Inflation, eating at his income, carries the threat of living in progressively showy "poverty." Like many solid citizens today, up to 80 percent of his take-home check may be tied up in fixed expenses. Cars, houses, boats, club memberships, and tuition for the children all cost more and more.

Arriving home tired and late, he is greeted by his wife, who has endured her own frustrations during the day. She bumped a fender car-pooling neighborhood youngsters to school. Their adolescent son was sent home from school for wearing his hair too long or having his clothes too dirty or something of the sort.

A student strike makes interesting reading in the suburban paper—complete with pictures of his son and the boy's peers carrying placards. The evening TV news picks it up as a quaint feature on life in suburbia, so he sees a few film clips—in living color—of the strikers arguing with the school principal. His son is out at a meeting of the protesters and therefore is not available for a fatherly talk.

On the way out to her meeting on the unfair treatment of women in our society, his wife informs him that his TV dinner is in the oven. She also mentions that their daughter, a college sophomore, wants to drop out of school and hitchhike through the West with two girlfriends. What she needs is enough advance financing from Dad to begin the trip.

If things work out right, he will have enough time and

energy left to gulp down the TV dinner, pay a few bills, and hop into bed early enough to rest up sufficiently to make the mad dash for the 7:15—who knows, it might actually leave on time tomorrow.

THE WORLD'S LONGEST PARKING LOT

Lest we think that the commuter who rides the train has all the fun, consider the special joys of driving bumper to bumper from suburban home to city office. Discounting such minor considerations as gasoline shortages, we can concentrate on matters like massive traffic tie-ups, fender-bender accidents, and frantic cutting in and out of traffic lanes.

Leaving the house a bit late, our mid-career hero hears the radio traffic helicopter announce that a gasoline tank truck has turned over at the intersection of two major expressways on his main route to an office meeting. Since there is a river of gasoline on the highway, the helicopter pilot announces that traffic into the city is being diverted along routes X, Y, and Z—the radio reception is garbled, but our driver manages to make out the route numbers. Unfortunately, he hasn't commuted over any of these routes for the past ten years and is uncertain about where to turn off to get to them.

Fortunately, he allowed himself an extra 45 minutes beyond his customary commuting time because he has an important meeting in one of his company's suburban offices this morning. There is hope of his reaching the meeting if he can take the right detours beyond the traffic tie-up spot. He stops at a gas station just off the expressway, which he thinks is somewhere near the right road. The young boy pumping gas lives 30 miles away and doesn't know enough about the local roads to be helpful.

However, our commuter knows that if he heads north and then east, he will swing back onto the expressway, he hopes at a clear point. By following the major traffic flow through the narrow, winding roads and stopping to ask directions from a local policeman, plus some dumb luck, he gets back on the expressway beyond the tie-up. He has to drive like an Indianapolis racer to make up for lost time and gets to his meeting with an upset stomach and heart palpitations, which he hopes are only temporary. Opening up his briefcase and pulling out a folder with papers, he gets ready to begin his managerial day.

A MOUNTAIN OF JUNK: STORAGE PROBLEMS IN THE AFFLUENT SOCIETY

Mid-career is a time when material possessions—homes, cars, lawn mowers and garden tools, clothes, recreational equipment, and the like—seem to proliferate. Sometimes a necessity and often a convenience, these goods are, however, also a measure of social status and achievement. But their care and feeding is a never-ending chore, and their housing is a nuisance.

With such a superabundance of the world's goods, the mid-career manager often finds himself without places to put them, so his garage becomes exclusively a storage area and he parks his car in the driveway. The number of bikes, lawn mowers, snow blowers, and pieces of sports equipment that can be packed into a suburban two-car garage is almost unbelievable. For today's mid-career manager, a former depression kid, this material abundance—albeit most of it is in need of repair—must be a perpetual source of amazement.

Those mid-career managers who have struggled with the special mystique of the aboveground family swimming pool can bear witness to life's vicissitudes with respect to material possessions. What with the neighbors' dogs digging holes under the pool area fence, near drownings, fist fights, children jumping gaily into the pool on the heads of swimmers, the wise pool owner keeps in close touch with his lawyer. In addition, relatives he scarcely knows have a way of suddenly reaffirming blood ties and family loyalties by coming over on weekends "to visit and see your lovely new pool that we've heard so much about."

Americans always seem to want to demonstrate their unique and special qualities and attainments through a display of worldly goods. Size and model of car, size of house and lot, landscaping and riding lawn mowers are visible signs of success. Some neighborhoods run a rat race in which each family tries to outdo the others in displaying its possessions. So each homeowner has to try harder each year just to keep up with the new gadgets and gimmicks that his neighbor purchases and displays.

WHY KIDS CAN'T TALK (OR LISTEN) TO THEIR PARENTS

Sociologists like Murray Milner point out that our society is, in many ways, polarized into three distinct subgroups. This polarization has a particular impact on the younger generation—the children of the mid-career manager. Milner sees these three groups as follows:

The Chosen. Usually the children of affluent parents, this group is dissatisfied with society in an idealistic sense. Many of them participated to some degree in the student riots of the late 1960s. They were protesting, as they saw it, the many flaws in our present society and its failure to attain the democratic ideal of the good life for all citizens.

The Excluded. This segment of society has been excluded, historically, from fair competition in the social race by virtue of having been born into socioeconomic groups that were given limited educational and economic opportunity.

The Vulnerable. This group, largely composed of people who are middle-aged or older, includes the majority of Americans who see themselves as having a personal stake in the present system. It further includes members of the upper class, the middle class, and the "respectable" working class; each class tries to get ahead within the system.

For a variety of reasons, many of the children of the *vulnerable* group in the late 1960s found themselves in the *chosen* category. As a rule, their parents had worked hard to give them educational and other opportunities they themselves had not had during the depression.

The parents were by then in their middle years—members of the producing generation whose efforts largely keep the wheels of society and industry turning. In their efforts to provide material things for career advancement, the parents usually had too little time for personal and recreational exchanges with their children.

Parents in the *vulnerable* group often found themselves under critical fire from their children, who were now in the *chosen* group through the parents' achievement efforts. The *vulnerables* have an obvious stake in the establishment and therefore, as their children see it, are directly responsible for many of the evils of contemporary society. Though many parents in mid-life agree with the criticisms of society and that much should be changed, they do not particularly enjoy being blamed for having caused or permitted these conditions. This type of accusation is particularly burdensome for the depression kid, now in mid-life, who worked hard and sacrificed to reach an economic level where he could provide his children with things he himself never had.

In Al, we have the case of a mid-career father who worked overtime as a manager in a growth company for many years. His son rejected the father's advice as well as his work-ethic values and refused to go on to college. After a year or so working in a gas station, the son changed his mind and sought his father's help. During a portion of the son's adolescent rebellions, however, interpersonal relationships between father and son were strained to the breaking point.

Al, in his own youth, had worked his way through college and gotten an engineering degree in a co-op program. It was therefore difficult for him to accept his son's values and attitudes during the son's dropout period after leaving high school.

DISRUPTION OF OLD CERTAINTIES

Social and technical changes of the 1950s and 1960s have done much to disrupt the old certainties that the mid-career manager of today can remember as having been part of his early life. During and after World War II, there was a good deal of consensus in America about such matters as patriotism, duty, commitment, and the value of following the Protestant-ethic code of work if one wanted to get ahead.

But today the manager in his own middle years can no longer count on those certainties to serve him as effective guidelines in making decisions or selecting options. In fact, many of the old certainties have been discredited to the point where it is difficult to know what larger beliefs the individual can hold with deep personal conviction. The devaluation of old values during the past 30 years has hit hardest in these areas:

Tradition disruption. Old traditions and slogans no longer have the ring of immutability and certainty. "My country, right or wrong," for example, may sound peculiar in a country in which American policy at both domestic and foreign levels has been under attack by many Americans. *The Ugly American,* a book that dealt with American images abroad, is a far cry from the older "my country, right or wrong" days. The relatively conservative mid-American life-style—which exists for many who live in the vast areas between the east and west coasts—has itself been questioned, challenged, and sometimes held up to ridicule.

Changes in fundamental values. Puritan pioneer values of thrift, patience, and perseverance are no longer considered worth much. The "now" generation says that it wants to live life to the full in the "here and now." We see college students dropping out, the rise of the counterculture with its rock music, drug use, and recreational sex all coming to the fore and challenging the older values.

National devaluation. To go from America as respected world leader in 1945 to the America of today, uncertain and engulfed in embarrassing national political scandals, is a painful shift in stature and image on the world scene within a brief period. Many of the serious cracks in the national picture have occurred just in the past five years.

American world leadership has crumbled. Its economic and political power are seemingly on the wane. Vietnam, with its disillusionments, brought a turning inward—a feeling that we should take care of our domestic problems and let the rest of the world look out for itself.

Loss of zest and optimism. All pioneer countries, with plentiful resources and open frontiers, tend to be optimistic about growth and progress. Open land in the American West added to the formation of a huge industrial society in this century kept this spirit of zest and optimism alive for over 150 years. Today things suddenly look disappointingly different. Doubts and uncertainty have replaced zest and optimism on our national scene.

Obsolescence of personal knowledge and skills. Technology changes so rapidly that the engineering graduate, for example, may find that much of what he learned in college has become obsolete within ten years or so after graduation.

Skills obsolescence is particularly evident in the career of the data-processing and computer-sciences manager in mid-career. If he attempts to keep up his "hands on" skills on third-generation equipment, he has difficulty in acquiring and maintaining his managerial expertise. At some point, the computer-sciences manager has to choose between becoming a management specialist and trying to keep up with the new technologies.

"Nothing works anymore." Each year we become increasingly dependent upon our mechanical gadgets to do things for us. With some exceptions, the old respect for craftsmanship and quality products seems to have vanished. The pages of *Consumer Reports* magazine are filled with letters to corporate executives from irate customers complaining bitterly about mechanical malfunction in expensive purchases. In a throwaway society, machines that last a long time and perform their specified functions effectively are almost anachronisms.

Pressures from overcrowding in mass urban society. There is presently at least one married-couples' organization whose members publicly state that they do not intend to have children. One reason they give is that of world population overcrowding. If current birth rates continue, present food technologies may not be able to keep up. The congestion and pressures of living in the large urban centers of America are available for all to see who want to look.

HOW TO COPE WITH THE SITUATION

Most of the pressures and stresses mentioned in this chapter have a strong impact on the mid-career manager. From urban crime to the junk piled high in his own garage, life presents him with too many problems, pressures, and decisions for comfortable living. In addition, many of the things he was raised to respect and to believe in deeply are being questioned, challenged, and devalued—almost on a day-to-day basis.

Yet these stresses and strains do not necessarily mean that all is lost. The problem and the challenge for the person in midlife is to see what is happening in new perspectives and to adjust both his personal perspectives and his habitual reactions to the new realities. This does not mean that he has to cast off his old beliefs en masse. On the contrary, much of what is new and contemporary is probably faddish and will not last. But some of the recent social and technical changes are here to stay. More are undoubtedly on the way. So the problem becomes one, as mentioned in *Future Shock,* of how to adjust intelligently to the new realities without going overboard and adopting every advertising fad that comes round the bend.

In Chapters 9 and 10 the mid-career manager will have an opportunity to systematically examine his present situation and to think about how best to get where he wants to go during the remainder of his business career.

THE MANAGER AS A SOCIAL ANIMAL

As many authors point out, man is essentially a social animal. We derive much of our satisfaction and reassurances in life from positive relationships with other people. While it is true that a complex urban-industrial society promotes alienation and aloneness, it is also true that meaningful and developmental two-way relationships can be generated if we possess the skills with which to generate them. Unfortunately, some organizational climates (entrepreneurial and bureaucratic) in which the manager often works and the suburban nuclear family life-style in which he often lives complicate the process of forming positive and meaningful interpersonal relationships.

Social Relationships with the Manager's Associates

In smaller communities, members of a company's managerial group tend to be thrown together quite a bit socially, usually because the community is limited in terms of people they consider their social and professional peers. In some cases, managers above a certain salary and status level are expected to be members of the local country club, boat club, or whatever, a requirement that is almost written into their job description.

In some company managerial groups, bridge clubs spring up. It becomes downright difficult for a manager to refuse an invitation to play bridge at vice-president X's home on Saturday evening, whether he feels like it or not. In smaller communities, where social relations are almost obligatory, there is often difficulty in keeping company politics out of informal social relations, and vice versa. A certain amount of in-company gossip is often exchanged at Saturday-night gatherings. If it gets back to the organization's grapevine in a distorted fashion, it can cause harm to a budding managerial career.

The newly arrived manager, his wife, and family have to use maze-bright analytical tactics to sort out the often unwritten protocol patterns that exist in the company he joins. Problems arising from distorted communications, particularly of the gossipy sort, can be ticklish. Old feuds, whether they are interpersonal or organizational (as between sales and marketing managers, for example), have to be dealt with in a circumspect manner. Newcomers try to be alert to avoid getting caught in the trap of taking sides with one faction or another.

In smaller communities deep in the boondocks, company togetherness often goes even farther than the Saturday-evening bridge game. In some companies, managers who belong to the same church form a habit of dropping by their offices on the way back from Sunday services to talk about fishing or golf while their wives are preparing lunch. These little group-membership-reinforcing social rituals are carefully observed by all in the community. They silently signify who is in and who is out of the various power cliques in that organization.

Another company phenomenon usually found in small communities is the plant manager or divisional president sitting at his desk on Saturday mornings, apparently poring over paperwork while actually he is holding court. He may or may not get much accomplished during these periods; however, there is an unconscious tendency for his key subordinates to drop into their own offices and clutter their desks with papers to prove to the boss that they are both loyal and busy. As a rule, the impromptu Saturday-morning meetings eventually transform themselves into informal bull sessions. More politically astute subordinates often find they can talk to the boss at such times in a way that enhances their promotional opportunities. Their chances are particularly good if the company does not have an effective management-by-objectives program on which to decide managerial performance contributions. Needless to say, the manager who does not form the habit of making himself available for such informal Saturday discussions and exchanges may run the risk of losing out when promotion time rolls around. Company picnics and parties in smaller communities are additional examples of semisocial associate relationships. Often in the small but rapidly growing organization, the management team has to work closely together for survival. Socializing is informal and casual. Lower-level managers speak casually to the board chairman or president because they know him well personally. As the organization gets larger, these old, informal contacts disappear. They are often replaced by more formal relationships as the organizational power structure and bureaucratic hierarchy become larger and more complex.

For most mid-career managers, building and maintaining meaningful social relationships with fellow managers requires a good bit of social and interpersonal skill.

Company Social Relationships in Larger Cities

The geography of urban-suburban living serves to limit social relationships among members of a company's managerial group who live in far-flung areas around a large urban center. In such areas, social relations tend to form more around membership in a college alumni group or a mutual hobby like golf, tennis, or boating than around the fact that people work for the same company.

Suburban neighbors often discover that they have common hobbies or interests and thus generate closer interpersonal and interfamily ties. Common concerns about crabgrass, landscaping, septic tanks, or local taxes often bring people together in the suburbs. Church or community groups for married couples are also vehicles for meeting people and establishing relationships.

Socializing with Relatives

Some families are relatively closely knit in terms of social friendships and interactions. In this respect, they are similar to the extended-family kinship groups of yesteryear, when grandparents, uncles, aunts, and cousins frequently got together for family sharings. In some ethnic groups, this type of family socializing becomes almost obligatory. In our present highly mobile society with its emphasis on the nuclear family (parents and children), much of the old sense of family extended-kinship relationships with their social get-togethers at holidays, vacations, and the like, have disappeared.

Social Relationships Within the Family

The American nuclear family we live in today has a variety of sharply defined, age-graded interests. As soon as the children enter school, their peer-group activities take over. Children who are inheritors of the affluent society often see their home as a sort of motel. They use it as a place in which to eat and sleep and change clothes. Sometimes they bring their friends over. During the adolescent period, children seldom do things with their parents unless the parents have a hobby such as camping that the children also enjoy.

The mid-career manager and his wife who were depression-born or depression-raised probably recall that there was considerably more intrafamily relating in the families they were born into than they find in the one they created. With telephones, bicycles, motor scooters, and small cars, children are infinitely more mobile today than were the children of the 1930s and '40s.

In the contemporary family, the wife often serves as chauffeur, car-pool director, baby-sitter, and part-time governess while children are young. The mid-career manager, in turn, often puts most of his energies into career and economic advancement. Current husband-and-wife role patterns all too frequently leave little time for interacting with the children on an informal, person-to-person basis.

By the time the manager and his wife have been married for 15 or 20 years, their urban-suburban life-styles may have drawn them to develop separate interests. Their interpersonal transactions can settle into a relatively unrewarding, unreinforcing set of predictable, boring patterns. Instead of mutual reinforcement and encouragement among members of nuclear families, we often find lack of communication and shared interests, which in turn can lead to indifference, alienation, and frustration.

Relationship Potentials in Mid-Career

Mid-career is a period in which the individual has to struggle with his or her personal feelings of doubt, disappointment, uncertainty, and regrets, feelings that he or she would like to explore with a close friend and confidant. Therefore, there is great value in exploring social relationships for their potential as a medium of exchange and growth.

Basically, positive and encouraging interpersonal relationships can do much for us at all stages of life. They can provide sharing, exchange, feedback, reassurance, and mutual appreciation. Our present high-technology urban society works against building such relationships, but they can be built by developing our skills for relating to people.

Deep friendships, either within or outside family and job relationships, depend upon the ability of both parties to be empathic. There has to be a sharing of feeling and concern. The relationship also ought to be reciprocal in that both parties gain in a mature manner.

Empathy and reciprocity do not mean that both individuals have to exchange in exactly the same way. For example, one party might get a great deal of personal satisfaction out of helping another explore his mid-career concerns and problems in a problem-solving way that leads to self-directed change. As Dr. Carl Rogers has indicated, empathic listening and a genuine concern for the other person as a human being are often the key factors in developmental interpersonal relationships.

The training and conditioning of many mid-career managers unfortunately has not provided them with empathic listening skills. Only recently have books been written on the coaching, counseling, and guiding aspects of boss-subordinate relationships on the job. Before that, the boss's role usually involved either the "tell" or the "tell and sell" approaches to communication that we discussed earlier. Neither of these managerial styles equips the manager for empathic sharing relationships.

Self-Exploration and Self-Disclosure
If the manager in mid-career is to take a close and careful look at himself, his problems, his concerns, and his opportunities with the help of a close personal friend, he has to do a certain amount of self-disclosing to that other person. This process is difficult for most of us who live in an essentially manipulative, promoter-

oriented society where inappropriate self-disclosure carries with it the possibility that the person with whom we share our concerns may use the information for gossip or for more subtle manipulations.

Building Interpersonal Competence

Regardless of the possible difficulties, good relationships can only be built through developing one's own ability to relate to others. Without good interpersonal relationships, we are condemned to go through life in essential loneliness and alienation. This condition, in turn, prevents us from gaining as much enjoyment as we could and should get from interaction with others and from life.

Interpersonal competence skills are learnable and perfectible with practice. Although the introvertive manager probably will always have more difficulty in developing these skills than the extrovertive type, the introvert can do much to improve his skills in relating positively and informally to people on a person-to-person basis.

For some managers, sensitivity-training courses have marked the beginning of their development in interpersonal skills. The manager who decides to use this approach should make certain that the sensitivity-training program he attends is conducted by competent psychologists or psychiatrists. Unfortunately, this is a field in which there is presently little or no state licensing and certification control. For this reason, care should be taken in selecting the program you attend. For other managers, reading at home is a good way to begin one's development.

Since positive, supportive, and developmental interpersonal relationships can become an important resource in helping the mid-career manager to understand himself and to begin a self-directed change and development action plan, interpersonal competence in the broad sense is a set of skills in which the manager can well afford to invest a good deal of time and effort. And they do take time and effort. Many of us raised in a high-technology, complex urban society often have to unlearn some of the old transactional patterns we acquired earlier in life. In addition, some of our negative self-images that might have developed over time may be in need of an overhaul.

Self-Awareness and Self-Analysis

Many of the vignettes we have reviewed so far are fine examples of mid-career managerial self-analysis. For example, Al, our first manager, decided through interaction sessions at a management training seminar to take a closer look at his compulsive workaholic life-style patterns. As a result of this self-analysis, he decided to change his managerial style so as not to work overtime. This decision, in turn, required him to polish up on his managerial skills of personal-time management and of delegation.

Frank, Mr. Troubleshooter, began to ask himself, after self-analysis in a group learning situation, why both he and the company always thought he was the only one to handle the tough crisis assignments on his job. After reflection, Frank decided to change his managerial style and to get out of the pressure cooker. Frank's health immediately improved, and his three hard-hitting subordinates, who were champing at the bit for more job responsibilities, were immediately happier as a result.

TYPICAL MID-CAREER PROBLEMS

Everyone who reaches the age associated with mid-career has to face certain typical problems. For some, these are traumatic. Others lack the skills to cope maturely and intellectually with their situations.

Rational approaches to problem solving and decision making help the mid-career manager to reach optimal solutions. Psychologists with a humanistic orientation take an essentially optimistic approach about people's abilities to deal with life situations as they come along. Behavior-modification specialists feel that intelligent individuals using a rational approach can do much to come out of mid-career with reasonable comfort and assurance. Good planning and foresight help. For example, Calvin, who bought a dude ranch at 53 and started a second career, possessed a great deal of relevant information about the ranch and ranch life before he made this move.

For other individuals, the emotional and personal aspects of their problems become more significant than the rational, problem-solving aspects. Particularly if a person has deep-rooted negative self-concepts or has strong anxieties and concerns about growing old in general, his emotional reactions to the changes that occur in mid-career may complicate his situation unduly. Bill, the "I'm not young anymore" manager, seemed to base a considerable portion of his sense of self-esteem and self-worth in his ability to compete successfully with younger men in sports contests. For him, reaching mid-career meant giving up some of the "winner" satisfactions he had known on his college athletic team.

Some of the problems that managers typically encounter in mid-career include:

Actual achievements compared to youthful aspirations. In youth we all dream about what life will be like and what we will achieve and accomplish. Our movies, novels, and television dramas are full of young heroes who achieve great heights through a combination of ability, charm, action, and wit.

If actual mid-career achievements go considerably beyond our youthful expectations, we can wind up feeling proud and happy. This is particularly true if we feel that our accomplishments were based on solid performance. On the other hand, if we feel we got by through luck or accident, we may always be somewhat anxious about achievement. A negative turn in our personal fortunes might wipe it all out.

Aligning achievements in terms of need satisfactions. Often our early achievement dreams have a strong fantasy component. We think we want to be a vice-president of a company to satisfy our needs. Actually, there are times when men work their way up to this job level in pursuit of achievement goals only to find that the requirements of the job do not meet underlying personal needs. As a consequence, we do not derive full job satisfaction from the work we are required to do every day.

Successfully coping with physiological changes. Even those mid-lifers who maintain an active physical-fitness program must face the fact that their energy reserves are not as great as when they were 20 years old. In our largely youth-oriented culture, such things as growing bald or having gray hair are considered signs of decay. Putting on too much weight or finding that we cannot swim or play tennis as well as we used to are other experiences that trigger the "I'm not young anymore" reaction. Compulsively hard-working "drivers" probably have the greatest difficulty in facing the physiological changes that usually occur in mid-career. They may continue to pressure their bodies for the same level of stamina and performance they got in early life. Carried to excess, this sort of personally induced pressure can result in physical disability.

Relationships. Competitively oriented managers often spend much of their lives trying to outdo those around them. Winning in the sense of getting more power, status, or money than associates becomes more difficult as we approach the ever-narrowing apex of the organizational pyramid. By mid-career, the overly avid achiever may have competed with others so often that he winds up with few friends and many organizational enemies.

Realizing that you have lived more than half of your life. By mid-career a person has to confront the reality that he has lived through more than half of his probable lifespan. In youth, the future seems to stretch endlessly ahead. In the teens, people who are over 20 seem old. In the twenties, anyone over 35 seems over the hill. From one's forties, retirement at 65 appears yet a tremendous way off. It is particularly in mid-career, however, that we come face to face with our mortality.

In addition, mid-life often becomes the period in which we review our career progress. Second careers after early retirement are increasingly frequent among today's managers. But to come out well, they must be planned for in mid-career. If no second-career prospects develop, then the manager has to think about what he is going to do with his time after he retires.

COMING TO GRIPS WITH PROBLEMS

Like the problems we encountered earlier in childhood, adolescence, and early adulthood, our mid-life problems can be easy or difficult, depending largely upon how we approach them. If the mid-career manager will avoid such typical pitfalls as those listed below, he should make his mid-career adjustment with relative ease:

Ignoring or postponing inevitable decisions. Successful retirement or second careers usually require advanced thinking and planning. Since we do not absolutely *have* to face these decisions in early mid-career, we are inclined to postpone them and to become overly absorbed in our current work situations. In some cases, postponing these decisions until late mid-life only reduces the number of alternatives and options available to us.

Low self-esteem or negative self-images. Excessive self-blame and self-criticism because one has fallen short of a youthful ideal can get us into a downward spiral of negative self-images. Because we deprecate ourselves unduly, we have less energy with which to cope with the real problems that confront us.

Irvin, the manager with a case of the bureaucratic blahs, is a man whose low sense of self-esteem may have compounded his feelings of being stuck in a comfortable situation but one that no longer challenged and stimulated him to achieve.

Unduly projecting resentments and hostilities onto others. Transactional analysts like Eric Berne label this playing games such as "If it weren't for you" or "If only it weren't for them." Projecting undue resentment and hostility onto others gives us an opportunity to blame them for our own failures and limitations. In the projection process, however, we continue to ventilate feelings rather than to take active, constructive steps to solve our problems.

Escape from immediate reality. Escape from monotonous or unpleasant everyday realities can take many forms. Daydreaming (the Walter Mitty type of fantasied successes) can prevent us from more effective action in the here and now. Overplanning, curiously enough, may wind up as another form of escape. When we spend a great deal of time getting ready for some intended action, we may never get around to actually executing our plans.

Concerns about what to do with the rest of one's life. Mid-career is a time when we can look back into the past and forward into the future. Often in mid-career the basic pressures of earning a livelihood, raising a family, and proving oneself to oneself and to the world have eased up a bit. Now we have more time for relaxation, for exploration, and for doing the things that are of greatest interest to us. Unfortunately, by the time we reach this mid-career plateau, our life-style and living habits may have hardened into a somewhat monotonous routine.

Often the mid-career manager's basic problem is how to look at himself and his life to date without the crust of long-formed habits and daily routines that have become almost automatic over the years. After he has examined his life, he may decide that his present life-style suits him pretty well and that he doesn't want to change very much at all. But in the process of self-analysis and acquiring self-awareness, he shouldn't become frozen into old patterns and old ways simply because they have become habitual over the years.

A thorough self-analysis requires that we step back far enough to generate useful perspectives on how we are currently operating today, how past events and circumstances impelled us in the direction we are currently following, and how our basic needs and interests in terms of job, career, interpersonal relationships, and our own talents and abilities can best be satisfied during the years that lie ahead.

SELECTED READINGS

Alvin Toffler, *Future Shock* (New York: Random House, 1970).

Murray Milner, *Columbia Forum* (spring, 1972).

Carl R. Rogers, *On Becoming a Person* (Oberlin College, The Nellie Heldt Lectures, 1954).

Sidney Jourard, *The Transparent Self* (New York: Van Nostrand Reinhold, 1971).

Joseph Luft, *On Human Interaction* (Palo Alto, Calif.: National Press Books, 1969).

Ernest G. Bormann et al., *Interpersonal Communication in the Modern Organization* (Englewood Cliffs, N.J.: Prentice-Hall, 1969).

George Robert Bach, *The Intimate Enemy* (New York: Morrow, 1969).

Thomas Gordon, *Parent Effectiveness Training* (New York: Wyden, 1970).

Muriel James, *Born to Win* (Reading, Mass.: Addison-Wesley, 1972).

8/Personal History: How Did You Get Here from There?

ALTHOUGH the mid-life stage is getting a great deal of attention these days, awareness of being middle-aged and even experiencing what some authors refer to as "the mid-life crisis" are not recent phenomena. The subject is simply being examined and discussed more now than before. Every individual who lives long enough goes, by definition, through mid-life.

In the past, psychologists put a good deal more emphasis on early and late childhood, adolescence, and early adulthood than they did on mid-life. Then old age was "discovered," and a great deal of psychological attention was put into studying individual adjustment as one got older.

EFFECTS OF ONE'S SOCIAL HISTORY

The social, economic, and political world into which an individual is born and the particular time span in which he lives obviously condition him in many ways. If he is born in an era of peace, prosperity, and growth, his life is apt to be relatively relaxed and fulfilling. But if he is born in an era of wars, famine, disease, or political and technological upheaval, he will grow up in a very different atmosphere. An individual born during the decline of Greece, the fall of the Roman Empire, or the Hundred Years War between France and England was likely to find a frustrating struggle for existence and survival his daily lot. The book *A Walk with Love and Death* provides a good example; it chronicles the tribulations of a young man and young woman who attempted to have a meaningful life together during the Hundred Years War.

Formative Events

Mid-career managers born in 1920, 1930, or 1940 had a special set of life experiences that conditioned their personalities and world outlook. The current mid-life generation has probably lived through an era of greater technological and social change than has any previous one. During the 40 or so years between 1930 and 1975, the degree and types of change that people experienced were so great as to warrant the label "future shock." In the first 20 years of that period, today's managers lived through the most severe depression in modern history, the most devastating war the world has ever known, and revolutionary new developments in transportation, communication, and computerized automation.

The nuclear age arrived. Science and technology held promise of the good life for all. Standards of living were high for most Americans. Increased urbanization brought more people into less space. Urban-suburban "strips" (Boston to Washington; Chicago to Pittsburgh; San Francisco to San Diego) heralded a new age in which increasingly large numbers of Americans crowded into increasingly smaller portions of the nation's available living space.

In the relatively short time span from 1945 to 1975, American prestige and influence declined considerably. The transition from an age of affluence, with a vista of never-ending growth and progress, to an age of uncertainty, with shortages, inflation, and political scandals that rocked the nation, took something like three decades. The fact of the decline of America's international influence was brought home emphatically to even the most stubborn optimists during the 1974 crisis brought on by export restrictions among the oil-producing nations.

Obliterated Landmarks

Given all this, it is small wonder if today's mid-career manager is somewhat shell-shocked and confused by what has taken place. Such deep and rapid changes loosen old cultural moorings, obliterate the fixed guideposts of our past, and wipe out trusted and familiar landmarks. They threaten old beliefs and familiar lifestyles. Behavior patterns learned in childhood are now in question.

Like Alfie, the existential nonhero of the movie of the same name, we often ask ourselves, "What's it all about?" What can possibly happen next? More important, we sometimes wonder if playing the game according to the old rules—conscientious employee, taxpayer, citizen, and parent—has really brought us the personal rewards and satisfactions we expected when we started out on our careers.

Without warning, the golden dream of an everlastingly affluent society has been abruptly shattered. The very abruptness of the change itself produced more doubts and uncertainties. How does one plan or intelligently forecast in his own life what might happen in the 1970s and 1980s?

ERIK ERIKSON'S APPROACH TO LIFE-HISTORY STAGES

Erik Erikson, a psychoanalytically oriented psychologist at Harvard University, combines Freudian life-stage analysis with social-anthropological concepts. The important life stages as Erikson sees them, and the crucial problems and developmental tasks usually associated with each stage, are discussed in the following subsections.

Birth to Age 1

At this stage, the infant struggles with the primary problem of *trust versus mistrust.* The baby is dependent upon his parents or on other adults for survival. Contacts with his mother in particular set the stage for the infant's interpretation of the world. If the mother creates, through her care and interaction with the child, the feeling that the world is a place that the child can trust, the child has a firm basic foundation on which to build his sense of self. Presumably his later feelings about interpersonal relationships are also strongly influenced by this early and basic interpersonal contact.

Depending upon the size of the child's family and the amount of time, energy, and interest the parents give to the very young child, his basic perceptions of self-worth and interpersonal relationships can begin to take a positive or a negative direction.

Ages 1 to 5

During this period, the child works at several key developmental tasks: learning to walk and to talk, to feed himself, to put on and take off clothes, and to control his elimination processes through toilet training. American middle-class mothers generally put a high premium of having their children complete these tasks as early as possible, parental pride getting involved in the child's accomplishments.

Autonomy versus self-doubt is the basic issue that confronts the child at this time in his life. If he masters these tasks easily and quickly, he is considered "smart," "advanced for his age," and a "good" child. If he is slow, inconsistent, and has difficulty doing these things according to the parents' time tables, he is sometimes considered less than adequate.

The successful performer reinforces his self-image as competent and autonomous in these specific ways. In later life, this self-confidence helps him to handle even more difficult problems. The early "unsuccessful" performer may always have deep underlying doubts about his ability to operate autonomously or to meet performance expectations.

Ages 5 to 7—Taking the Initiative

At this stage, most children can communicate and move about on their own. Their world expands into play in the yard or the park. They begin to have friends and to be more on their own. To the child, this is the age of experimentation and for expanding his initiative. He jumps on things, runs, falls, pushes, and dives. In the process, he is bound to break things and to cause adults, including his parents, some inconvenience.

If the parents encourage action and initiative, the child is likely to grow up with confidence in his ability to solve life's problems through independent individual "doing." On the other hand, if he is strongly criticized or blamed for his activities, he may grow up with much self-doubt regarding his ability to take successful independent action. Such deep self-doubt may inhibit his leadership efforts and thereby cause him to spend his life in an essentially follower role.

Ages 8 to 14—The School Years

Though prekindergarten and nursery schools now push the school-entering age below eight and high school and college extend it beyond age 14, the 8-to-14 period is that in which the child is "processed" by our compulsory (public or private), state-supported educational system. In school, the child competes intellectually with his peers on tasks assigned by teachers. If he is a good student—either bright in the sense of grasping required subject matter quickly or likable in the sense of pleasing teachers and having good peer relationships—he is likely to get by this period without much difficulty. Unfortunately, much elementary education is still based on rote memorization and the recitation-regurgitation method popular in the 1800s. Children who alertly conform to the elementary school's essentially bureaucratic structure generally get adequate or better grades and are considered "bright."

Suburban elementary schools have the advantage of a high tax rate, somewhat lower pupil-teacher ratios, newer classrooms, audio-visual aids, and other equipment. However, the learning process is still so strait-jacketed by educational custom that the curious, the innovative, and the honestly bored (with subject matter taught in an uninspired manner) often have difficulties getting even average grades. Each type of nonconforming child threatens the system in a somewhat different way.

Current polls of college students indicate that while they did not always like their earlier elementary and secondary school experiences, they have resigned themselves to playing the establishment educational game—as adults define and control it—in order to earn the educational trading stamps that will give them access to good-paying jobs in the future.

In our high-technology society, children who do poorly in their school work during this 8-to-14 age period almost inevitably suffer a serious handicap in their later careers. This is because success in a technical or professional career is highly dependent upon success in formal education.

Ages 15 to 21—Adolescence

In adolescence, many are confronted with a number of difficult choices and adjustment problems. Working out a clear-cut sense of identity, who one is as an individual and not merely as an appendage of the family one was born into, is one key task of people in this age group. Developing a coherent ego—a sense of self, who one is, what one wants to become and to do with one's life—is a difficult task for most in our high-technology urban society.

Some young people develop an early sense of vocational conviction and prepare themselves through formal education in a smooth manner. However, statistics indicate that about 40 percent of the entering freshman classes in one of the country's best universities no longer earn their bachelor's degree within the 'traditional four-year period. This would indicate a substantial degree of young adult dissatisfaction with our present educational system and the lock-step implications that they should go immediately from late adolescence into early adulthood as a disciplined member of society without having spent much time in living along the way.

Choosing between intimacy and alienation and loneliness is another developmental dilemma that young people of this age struggle with, according to Erikson. How to form deep and emotionally meaningful relationships with members of one's own sex as well as with the opposite sex is the task. Indications are that the typical young adult of today adopts a "transient" strategy in his interpersonal relations with members of the opposite sex more often than the more traditional pattern. The transients stay loose, postpone marriage, and generally have several relationships of varying degrees of intimacy before settling down. In contrast, the traditionals often start dating in high school and wind up getting married as soon as they are legally of age.

Erikson's point is that if we go through the life stages in a relatively comfortable manner, our success at each stage reinforces our self-confidence and our sense of ability to master the environment. This confidence and sense of mastery, in turn, equip us to handle the usually more difficult problems we run into in middle and later life.

A MANAGER BORN IN 1930

When the concept of the effects of particular early-life experiences on a person's later life was discussed with Erick, he said, "Boy, are you singing my song. I was born in London in 1930. I can't remember too much about my early life, but I vividly remember being evacuated from London as the war got worse. We lived in the country for about five years. They were good years in many ways. Country life is a wonderful change for a city kid. But young as we were then, we children realized the seriousness of the war.

"When I was fourteen, we returned to London to find much of it bombed out. All sorts of family adjustments had to be made. When I finished high school, I emigrated to the United States and did a hitch in the American army. Afterward, I went to Harvard Business School. I remember looking out at the commuter traffic pouring into Boston in the mornings along Storrow Drive and making up my mind I was never going to get caught up in the corporate rat race. I guess that's why I've been in teaching and consulting ever since."

A MANAGER BORN IN GERMANY

Floyd had an even more traumatic childhood. As a ten-year-old boy in Germany when the Russians were advancing on Berlin at the end of World War II, he remembers helping pick people out of the rubble created by shelling and bombing the previous night. Food and other bare essentials were scarce—he barely managed to survive. Being bright and ambitious, he managed to get to America and acquire an education in the computer field. He now manages the computer operation for a large financial complex.

The experiences of his early years left their mark on Floyd. He is, in mid-career, a loner and highly anxious because he fears that his comfortable upper-middle-class life may be interrupted by some unknown catastrophe. His wife, also a refugee, is also a loner. The two of them have few friends, are almost completely isolated from social contacts, and find it difficult to be outgoing, warm, and friendly with their suburban neighbors.

On the job, Floyd keeps his guard up at all times. He is resentful, anxious, and suspicious. He fears that his superiors may take advantage of him. He is also a poor delegator. In the first place, he communicates poorly. It takes some time for subordinates to find out exactly what he means when he gives instructions. Though he speaks English competently, his interpersonal style remains guarded and cryptic. His anxiety about what doom might occur if things went wrong pressures him to hover over his assistants to make certain they are completely error-free. The assistants resent Floyd's style; consequently, the turnover among his key subordinates is higher than it is in similar units in the corporation.

Unless Floyd can restructure his interpersonal transactional style through insight and behavior modification, he probably won't be promoted to a higher responsibility. Though his superiors recognize his intellectual ability, his limitations as a managerial leader limit his further career opportunities.

DANIEL LEVINSON'S STUDY: LIFE DEVELOPMENT OF PEOPLE IN MID-CAREER

Professor Daniel Levinson of Yale University has applied social-psychological and social-anthropological concepts to a study of a number of individuals going through the mid-career period. He uses an analytical model similar to that of Erik Erikson. Among the things Levinson emphasizes in his study are the life-stage activities and problems described in the following subsections.

Ages 16–22—Pulling Up Roots

Here the individual is dealing with problems associated with breaking away from his family and becoming an individual in his own right. Often economically dependent on his parents if he is in college, he wants to break away and become his own man. He is usually eager to find his own place in life and to prove his personal competence.

The young person who succeeds in handling the problems associated with this life stage goes on to subsequent stages with comfort and confidence. Those who don't may become permanent dropouts from a society that they were unable to fit into.

Ages 22-29—Provisional Adulthood

At this stage the young person finishes formal education and begins to establish himself in the world. Career success and the formation of intimate relationships with others are the main tasks here. If the individual has specific vocational interest and has developed relevant skills, he usually moves into a job and career area early. Like many individuals brought up in our complex society with its economic fluctuations, however, he may shop around and try a number of different jobs before his career goals firm up.

Ages 29-32—A Transition Period

During these years the individual is likely to look back at what he has or has not done so far. His self-evaluation can prompt him to continue along the same route—if he is satisfied with what he sees. If not, he may make major changes. He may move into other fields or go back to school for further education. If he is dissatisfied with marriage and family, he may separate or get a divorce. In general, this is a period of life review and often of an abrupt change from one's previous life-style.

Ages 32-39—Settling Down

The period between ages 32 and 39 is often one of intense concentration on job and career advancement. A great deal of the manager's time and effort are spent in proving himself in the competitive adult world. In many cases, the manager becomes quite single-minded in pursuit of this goal. As he does so, his social contacts tend to be reduced—he deliberately cuts himself off from the outer world to a great extent. Old friendships are often dropped or are minimally maintained at this time.

The assistance of a "mentor," an older man (usually 6 to 20

years older) than the manager, is often helpful to the younger man in the career period between ages 32 and 39. The older man acts as an interested "sponsor" and assists the younger man in getting ahead. He may also impart his own experience and wisdom to the younger man.

Managers who do not easily show deference to authority and who have rebelled against their own fathers and mothers as authority figures often have difficulty fitting into a mentor relationship at this stage in their careers. As a result, they lack the advantages of such a relationship at a crucial stage in their career development. It is possible for the manager of this age period who has difficulty with older authority figures to alter his interaction style with such men in time to gain the potential benefits such relationships may contain. Orville, the manager who was able to resolve an authority-relationship conflict in his first job after receiving his M.B.A. degree, is a manager who did this well.

Ages 39–43—The Potential "Mid-Life Crisis" Period

This is the transitional period in which a "mid-life crisis" develops if one is to develop at all. Like the earlier period of life review, the manager in the 39–43 age period is apt to review his life for a second time. If he finds that all is going well, he tends to continue on course with optimism and effectiveness. However, this is the period in which the gap between one's early dreams of achievement are most likely to run directly into the realities of what he has actually done.

When this gap becomes too great, feelings of resentment, disappointment, and frustration can and do become very obvious. This is often the time when we see the presumably successful and satisfied manager kick over the traces and do things that are quite alien to his previous life-style. The executive dropout and the mid-life hippie are two examples of this abrupt life-style shift.

In some cases, a life switch at this point has a long-term negative effect on the manager's career. He may choose to throw away a number of years of seniority and acquired expertise to go chasing after the will-o'-the-wisp of his dream job. However, in still other cases, such a career shift turns up underutilized or underdeveloped skills and interests.

Many managerial mid-career transition periods have a very positive and self-enhancing outcome. During the 39–43 age span the mid-career manager often has an opportunity to catch up with himself. He is apt to gain additional organizational and professional recognition for his accomplishments, which often comes through promotion. Even if he does not move to the top tiers of his profession, advancement opportunities are still a distinct possibility.

In addition, his social position in the community often enhances his sense of self-worth as a member of society. On the job he usually acquires increasing organizational powers based on expertise and judgment gained through experience. In most cases, his physical drive and energy levels are still high. All in all, he lives in a relatively comfortable world.

Ages 43–50—The Re-establishing and Flowering Period
This is apt to be a period of both stabilization and contentment. His family and marital relationships often become more rewarding. In those instances where his children give promise of attaining success through competent performance, he can, in a sense, pass the torch along to them and take pride in their life accomplishments. He has more free time and often more spendable income available for travel, hobbies, and self-development than he had in the years when his family was growing up.

In this stage of his life, the manager is often involved in working his way out of the feelings of isolation and aloneness that are common to people living in an urban-suburban high-technology society. Having only a nuclear family rather than an extended family with kinship ties, the manager comes to realize that more people in our time go through life with an essential sense of aloneness than was the case in the rural-agricultural era with extended family relationships and close neighborhood and community ties.

The manager has to come to grips with his competitive achievement strivings if these are strong motivating factors for him. In many cases, he also has to learn how to relate to others on a more relaxed, personal friendship basis. He must strive to break down isolation barriers and to find, develop, and enjoy deeper interpersonal sharings and exchanges. Accepting his own "expressive" needs, his underlying desire to express feelings and sentiments has to be rethought after years of relatively unsentimental, task- and dominance-oriented behavior used in work relationships on the job.

Like Professor Erikson, Professor Levinson, in his current studies at Yale, indicates that what occurs in these various life stages (roughly from ages 16 through 50) is important to the mid-career manager's later personal and job satisfactions. When he handles the problems commonly associated with each stage in a positive and intelligent manner, the successes obtained along the way make him more likely to succeed in the future.

If he still has some unresolved problems and concerns left over from previous stages in his life, mid-career is an excellent time to work them through in a way that promises maximum potential for an ultimately successful outcome.

EFFECTS OF FAMILY PATTERNS ON PERSONALITY DEVELOPMENT

In many ways, we are truly products of the era in which we live. In many other ways, we are also products of the family into which we were born and raised.

The father's work tends to define the family's socioeconomic status. In America, children from wealthy upper classes have different life experiences from children born into lower-class families. Income from the father's work—and increasingly from the mother's work in a dual-career family—determines a certain standard of living. The latter is, in turn, influenced by the geographical area one lives in, the size and type of home one has, and the kinds of schools one goes to. Neighborhoods and social activities put the individual in contact with certain types of peers on the playground, on the athletic field, and in school.

The family's belief system tends to shape personal values and beliefs. If a family is conservative politically, the children tend to be conservative. If it is warm and outgoing, so are its members. When a family is studious and intellectually inclined, the children tend to be influenced in that direction.

Parental Influences

In some families the father is studious and aloof. In others he is interested in athletics and hunting and fishing. In still others he is gregarious, outgoing, and highly social. Some mothers are efficient, neat, and good money managers, taking pride in bringing their children up in the conventional middle-class way of life. Other mothers are disorganized and relatively ineffectual as parents. Still others are highly social and spend much of their time at club meetings and bridge parties.

Our mother's and father's individual life-styles, whatever they may be, are bound to have many influences on our own childhood and adolescent experiences. Some families remain in one place—they may live in one house for decades. Others, often the families of business executives, move around a lot as the father's career development dictates job transfers.

Family Interaction Patterns

The types of family interaction patterns that the growing child experienced in early life are of particular influence. Transactional analysis authors such as Murial James place special emphasis on interpersonal family interaction patterns as determinants of our later life behavior. Transactional students feel we can often benefit from a thoughtful analysis of our early life stages in terms of:

☐ The basic traits and physical factors we were born with. Some babies are large, others are small; some are active and outgoing at birth, while others are silent or may have physical disabilities.

☐ The types of family interaction patterns we were exposed to or the interpersonal climate of family we were raised in.

☐ The possible effects of both of the above on our self-perception and on our interpersonal relationship pattern in later life. Mid-career, in particular, is a good time to look at the possible effects of early life on our present behavior and successes or failures.

Family climates or interaction patterns can be analyzed in the following ways.

The nurturing and rewarding family. This family is probably the ideal insofar as the child's successful development through early life stages is concerned. Children are emotionally supported and are encouraged to develop their interests and abilities. They get positive feedback on the things they do well. Such feedback enhances self-esteem and self-confidence.

The ambivalent family. Mixed emotional reactions are typical of this family. Depending upon the parents' moods, the child may be nurtured and rewarded or he may be criticized, neglected, or ignored. This type of climate makes the child uncertain about praise and punishment for his activities in later life.

The judgmental family. Family interaction here centers around criticizing and judging the behavior of younger members. Usually there is only one "right way" for children to behave. Deviations from accepted patterns bring criticism. The child often "judges" his own way through life. He tends to set rigid, uncompromising standards for himself and others. He resents and condemns any life-styles or other behavior that falls outside these prescribed boundaries.

The manager who comes from a *judgmental* family background may be particularly hard on himself if his actual achievements have not measured up to his earlier youth expectations. He may do a lot of self-blaming, or he may project his failures and limitations onto others as a way of escaping direct personal blame.

The critical and negative family. Somewhat different from the judgmental family, the prevailing world view and expectations in the critical family are those of pessimism and concern over probable failure. Children grow up feeling that the cards are stacked against them. Their habit of finding the negatives in a situation prevents them from being positive in their approach to life opportunities. As a consequence, their career attainments often fall short of their basic potential.

The indifferent family. The child raised in this family climate grows up feeling that no one cares very much about him personally. Often he is provided with material satisfactions. In some wealthy families with an indifferent climate, the parents are preoccupied with their own interests and activities, and they turn the children over to well-paid governesses or maids. The child's basic interpersonal contacts are then strongly influenced by the governess or maid. These children tend to grow up indifferent to people in the world they live in because their parents were basically indifferent to them.

The sterile family. This is more a collection of individuals who share a common roof than it is a family in the complete sense. For one reason or another, adults in this type of family are incapable of giving much warmth or encouragement to their offspring.

The mid-career manager raised in a sterile family may find that he is repeating this pattern with his own children. Should he desire to change his interpersonal style with members of his own family, he can do so. He will have to do a considerable amount of self-analysis, however, to discover the underlying reasons for his present style of behavior. In all probability, he will also have to unlearn some of the old transactional patterns he acquired in childhood before he can learn new, better-relating types of patterns.

APPLYING THE LEVINSON MODEL TO A TYPICAL MID-CAREER MANAGER

In Chapter 9 the reader will be asked to develop a mid-career balance sheet using the materials in the first seven chapters as a guideline. Before we move on to this exercise, it will be useful to apply Professor Daniel Levinson's mid-life model to a brief general case analysis to consider the major social, political, and economic events of our time in relation to the various life stages that a hypothetical manager might well have traversed.

The experience will be somewhat different depending upon when the manager was born, because so many social and technological events have taken place in the past 25 years. Prior to 1950, for example, there was little or no television available for American viewers. In 1975, many families have two or more sets in the home.

The manager born in 1920 would be 55 in the year 1975, one born in 1930 would be 45, and one born in 1940, 35. Each of these men would have had a somewhat different personal life experience based on the times in which they were at certain life stages. Choosing a midpoint, let us look at the developmental life stages of a manager born in 1930.

Ages 16 to 22 (1946 to 1952)

The Yale studies indicate that this is the life stage in which the individual is growing away from his family. His key problems are those of establishing an independent identity and of developing a satisfactory degree of intimate relationships with other people.

For Americans, this was the period of the post-World War II boom and also of the Korean War. Thousands of World War II veterans returned to college campuses, and the educational boom was on in earnest. Jobs were relatively plentiful. Our manager between ages 16 and 22 was probably concerned with the choice between getting an early job start and continuing on in formal education. If he chose the college route, he was busy studying. If he opted for an early job life, he was getting started in the work world. Major strikes in steel and coal in 1949 brought a temporary recession, but this was offset by the Korean War arms buildup that began in 1950.

The manager who was then over 18 might well have been drafted into the Korean War. Unlike World War II, the national climate surrounding the Korean conflict did not contain elements of fervent patriotism. It was a difficult war to understand. While our manager may have been drawn into it, his peers in college or on the job may have remained safely at home. They were not required to make the personal sacrifices that he made. The war itself held little glory. Returning Korean War veterans were anxious to resume their civilian lives as soon as they were mustered out.

Ages 22 to 29 (1952 to 1959)

During this life stage, the individual is concerned with getting into the adult world. The Korean War veteran may have gone back to college during this period to complete his education. If he followed the traditional pattern, he probably got married early. He also may have gotten a job with one company and stayed with it. If he took the transient pattern, on the other hand, he may have remained unmarried and tried several jobs with different companies. The transient would use this period primarily for looking around and exploring career opportunities.

Ages 29 to 32 (1959 to 1962)

This is often a period of early-life transition. The married, locked-in traditionalist tends to review his job and family commitments. He may kick over the traces in one or both areas and follow an opposite life-style pattern. The traditionalist who sees himself as locked in may become restless and dissatisfied in this phase of his life. The 30-year-old transient, on the other hand, may decide to settle down and catch up with his peers in terms of job stability and family development.

For America, 1959–1962 were the "Camelot" years when John Kennedy was President. Fresh new hopes were springing up. Younger men were taking charge in government and business, men who were bright, active, and articulate. With continued business expansion, jobs were plentiful and career-mobility opportunities were in good supply.

Ages 32 to 39 (1962 to 1969)

This is the period in which the manager settles down into organizational life. He works hard at career advancement. Many men become fanatically preoccupied with work effort at this time, so concentrating on career that they narrow their outside interests and contacts.

In the nation, the 1962–1969 period covered the transition from the Kennedy years to Johnson's Vietnam struggle and onward into the Nixon era. The Vietnam War stimulated the economy and provided organizational growth with concomitant career advancement potentials.

This was also the era in which national disillusionment and deep divisions between younger and older generations surfaced. On the campus, protest marchers picketed; in some institutions, buildings were burned. Political conventions were terrorized. Police, as viewed on television, clubbed youthful violators as they put them into paddy-wagons. The nation's sense of security began to fall apart. The national debt mounted, the seeds of runaway inflation were planted.

Ages 39 to 43 (1969 to 1973)

Developmental psychologists see this stage as one of late mid-life transition when the manager is inclined to re-evaluate his life to date. If satisfied, he tends to continue doing what he has been doing. If he is deeply dissatisfied, however, this is the age when he may drop what he has been doing and turn to something else. He might feel that he has only one more opportunity in life to do the things he wants to do. Consequently, many mid-career managers switch from their old life-styles and patterns to try out something new.

Nationally, this was the period in America when mounting hostility toward the Vietnam War with its budget drains generated heavier internal resentments. The 1969–1971 recession caused a higher-than-usual percentage of layoffs, particularly in the aerospace and electronics industries. During the recession, managerial promotional opportunities declined appreciably for the first time in many years.

This was also the period in which investigative reporters like David Halberstam and Jack Anderson were printing exposés of highest-level government blunderings and even of media manipulations in which the American people were deliberately given erroneous information by their government. The earliest of the Watergate exposés added to national confusion and discontent. The Vietnam War settlement, growing inflation, and the beginnings of food, raw materials, and energy shortages at home combined to create further uncertainties.

Ages 43 to 50 (1973 to 1980)

Psychologists find, through their studies, that this is often the golden era of mid-career. In most cases, by this time the manager's personal career will have gone well. His family life is usually on an even keel. His children have grown up or are nearly grown. He has probably arrived in terms of job and career success. He has a home in the suburbs, if he wants one, and a relatively high degree of job and community status.

Even though others see him as having arrived, he still has to face the problems associated with essential aloneness that so frequently characterize our urban-technological world. Even though his marriage may be a stable one, he is not sure that any other individual, no matter how close, will ever really understand his deeper thoughts and feelings. Despite friends and relatives, in our essentially egocentric world with its peripheral interpersonal contacts he may not get as much satisfaction from relationships as he wants.

YOUR PRESENT MID-CAREER SITUATION

Because mid-career in the contemporary world can easily occupy 20 or more of the manager's most fruitful and potentially satisfying years, it is an excellent time for him to take a look at the kinds of considerations we have covered so far in terms of his own life. If he is now in early mid-career, the concepts expressed will help him anticipate the types of situations he is apt to encounter within the next few years.

If he is in the middle of the mid-career stage, he can use the perspectives developed in the book as a guideline for planning the kind of future he desires. If he is in later mid-career, he can catch up on what has happened and what is now happening to him in a way that will enable him to acquire the techniques and tools for planning his future.

SELECTED READINGS

Hans Koningsberger, *A Walk with Love and Death* (New York: Simon & Schuster, 1961).

Erik H. Erikson, "Growth and Crises of the 'Healthy Personality,'" *Symposium on the Healthy Personality* (New York: Josiah Macey, Jr., Foundation, 1950).

For a well-written summary of Professor Daniel Levinson's research at Yale University, see Gail Sheehy, "Catch-30: And Other Predictable Crises of Growing Up Adult," *New York Magazine* (February 18, 1974).

9/Setting Up Your Mid-Career Balance Sheet

THE EARLIER chapters of this book are designed to serve as an outline and guide in helping you to develop your own Mid-Career Balance Sheet. The road to useful self-understanding comes through a careful self-analysis of (1) where you are in your managerial career at this time and (2) which key events in your past life were most influential in generating your present life-style and your perceptions of yourself and the world.

GENERATING QUANTIFIABLE DATA FOR SELF-ANALYSIS

Several things about your past life are quantifiable. For example, your salary increases will give you feedback on your career advancement. So will the number of promotions you have had in the past five or ten years. And so will the various responsibility levels you have reached during this same five- or ten-year period.

Personal Impressions and Estimates

While some of your life-history information can be quantified in a useful way, other portions will best be looked at on the basis of your own impressions and estimates. Being objective about oneself and about the impressionistic aspects of one's life-history information is obviously the chief problem.

If we are inclined toward rationalization or projection or both, we may wind up playing the games Eric Berne called "If it weren't for them" or "If it weren't for it"—"it" being a significant event in your life. Probably none of us can ever be completely objective about his own life-history information. On the other hand, it is possible for us to organize this type of information as objectively as possible. On the basis of this organization we can then proceed toward self-analysis for the purpose of self-development and *self-directed change* in our mid-career period.

Using Others as Co-evaluators

After you have generated your own data in setting up your Mid-Career Balance Sheet, you may want to share some or all of it with friends. As mentioned in Chapter 5, friends can often be helpful in providing an outsider's perspective on the meanings of our analysis. Criteria for selecting a co-evaluator should include the following:

☐ The person selected will treat your material as confidentially as you want him to.

☐ He or she is interested in being helpful as a sounding board in your self-analysis process.

☐ Preferably, the person you select has had sufficient related life experiences (usually a function of age by having lived up to or through the mid-career stage or else by being a mature younger individual) to understand and offer useful comments on the material you decide to share.

☐ Ideally, the person would also have sufficient coaching, counseling, and guidance skills of the sort now being taught in managerial-skills courses to provide you with appropriate types and forms of feedback. It should be presented in ways that enable you to reflect on the feedback and use it operationally in setting up your Action Plan.

DETERMINING YOUR LIFE-SATISFACTION INDEXES

A good approach to setting up your Mid-Career Balance Sheet is in terms of an overall Life-Satisfaction Index. Most of us are more satisfied with some key aspects of mid-career than with others. As one reviews his life up to this point, however, he is usually able to give it an overall rating in life satisfaction.

On the following nine-point scale, circle your present life-satisfaction score as you see it:

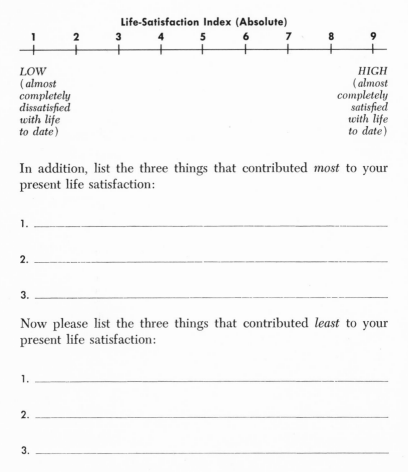

Life-Satisfaction Index (Absolute)

| 1 | 2 | 3 | 4 | 5 | 6 | 7 | 8 | 9 |

LOW
(almost
completely
dissatisfied
with life
to date)

HIGH
(almost
completely
satisfied
with life
to date)

In addition, list the three things that contributed *most* to your present life satisfaction:

1. _____

2. _____

3. _____

Now please list the three things that contributed *least* to your present life satisfaction:

1. _____

2. _____

3. _____

The foregoing Index was an absolute rating of your life satisfaction. To determine your Life-Satisfaction Index on a comparative basis, please complete the following sentence:

I feel I am about as satisfied as the following percentage of the people I know whose careers are similar to mine (circle one):

10%   20%   30%   40%   50%   60%   70%   80%   90%

DETERMINING YOUR JOB'S REWARDS AND BENEFITS

Self-Analysis Chart 1 lists what many mid-career managers consider to be the most important benefits or rewards associated with their job. Consider each item in terms of your present job and consider whether it is very definitely a plus, somewhat of a plus, relatively neutral, somewhat of a minus, or definitely a minus. After you have checked the appropriate columns in Chart 1, please answer the questions that follow.

Self-Analysis Chart 1. Rewards and benefits of your job.

ITEMS FOR EVALUATION	Definite plus $++$	Somewhat plus $+$	Neutral 0	Somewhat minus $-$	Definite minus $--$
1. Pay level	___	___	___	___	___
2. Status level	___	___	___	___	___
3. Opportunity for recognition	___	___	___	___	___
4. Opportunity for achievement	___	___	___	___	___
5. Opportunity to develop your full capacities	___	___	___	___	___
6. Challenge—the job pushes you to use your full resources and abilities.	___	___	___	___	___
Self-analysis subtotals	___	___	___	___	___

In terms of those rewards and benefits of my present job, I feel that the two greatest pluses are:

1. _____

2. _____

I feel that the two areas that need the most developing or change are:

1. _____

2. _____

DETERMINING YOUR MANAGEMENT SKILLS

How well do your present skills as a professional manager qualify you for your present job? Rate yourself on these skills in Self-Analysis Chart 2.

Self-Analysis Chart 2. Your management capacities and skills.

ITEMS FOR EVALUATION	Definite plus + +	Somewhat plus +	Neutral 0	Somewhat minus −	Definite minus − −
1. Personal effectiveness skills					
A. Time management	____	____	____	____	____
B. Decision making	____	____	____	____	____
C. Delegation	____	____	____	____	____
2. Interpersonal effectiveness skills					
A. Ability to manage 1-to-1 relationships	____	____	____	____	____
B. Ability to manage effectively in small-group situations	____	____	____	____	____
3. Administrative effectiveness skills					
A. Handling organizational paperwork	____	____	____	____	____

Self-Analysis Chart 2 continued.

	+ +	+	0	–	– –
B. Using organization's systems effectively	——	——	——	——	——
C. Handling budgets and costs	——	——	——	——	——
D. Coordinating	——	——	——	——	——
4. Technical effectiveness skills					
A. Ability to solve difficult problems in my technical field	——	——	——	——	——
B. Ability to help my subordinates solve difficult problems in my technical field	——	——	——	——	——
Self-analysis subtotals	——	——	——	——	——

In terms of my capacities and skills relative to my present job, I feel my two greatest strengths are:

1. _____

2. _____

I feel my two greatest development-need areas are:

1. _____

2. _____

DETERMINING YOUR PRESENT EFFECTIVENESS AS A MANAGER

How effectively do you feel you operate in your present organization? Have you in the past and do you now effectively handle (1) major technical-systems changes and (2) social-systems (people) changes that have come along in your organization during the past five or ten years? How well do you understand the organizational dynamics that underlie the present climate of your organization? Self-Analysis Chart 3 should help you to answer those questions.

Self-Analysis Chart 3. Your effectiveness in the organization.

ITEMS FOR EVALUATION	Definite plus ++	Somewhat plus +	Neutral 0	Somewhat minus −	Definite minus − −
1. Maze brightness					
A. Understand my present organizational climate (e.g., entrepreneurship, bureaucracy, fast growth, professionally managed) and work well within it.	____	____	____	____	____
B. Understand how the *influence* networks operate, and work well within them.	____	____	____	____	____
C. Understand how the *decision-making* networks operate, and work well within them.	____	____	____	____	____
2. Goal achievement					
A. Ability to achieve assigned organizational goals	____	____	____	____	____
B. Ability to lead my subordinates in achieving goals	____	____	____	____	____
3. Managing change					
A. Managing technical changes	____	____	____	____	____
B. Managing people changes	____	____	____	____	____
Self-analysis subtotals	____	____	____	____	____

In terms of my personal effectiveness in my present organization, I feel my two greatest strengths are:

1. _____

2. _____

I feel my two greatest development-need areas are:

1. _____

2. _____

EVALUATING YOUR CAREER ACHIEVEMENTS AND SATISFACTIONS

Career achievements and satisfactions are both *relative* and *absolute*. For example, you can compare your actual career attainments to your career ambitions, which would be a relative measure of career achievement. Or you could checklist yourself at a specific level on your company's organizational chart, such as manager, director, vice-president, president, and so forth. This would be an absolute measure of your career achievements in terms of organizational title and status.

When we evaluate our own career progress in terms of our career ambitions, capabilities, and opportunities, we usually think in the following terms:

☐ How far up the career ladder have I come from the level at which I started?

☐ How long did this take me? In terms of advancement in this organization, was it very fast, fast, average, somewhat below average, or definitely below average?

☐ What factors have been most crucial to my career advancement to date?
Performance. Recognition for results.
Conformity. Fitting into organizational role expectations.
Relationships. Having positive relationships with those who can help my career advancement.
Readiness. Being ready for advancement.
Availability. Being in the right place at the right time.

☐ How effectively have I developed my career skills as I went along?
Very well developed. I can handle present job with ease and am qualified to handle at least one step up the ladder.

Well developed. I can handle present job with relative ease. Might be able to handle next step up.

Adequately. I am as well qualified as most of the people at my job level.

Some gaps—not serious. I realize that I have some skill gaps— there are key things about my present job that I should improve on.

Gaps—serious. Though I am doing this job, I realize that there are one or more key skill gaps that I should take immediate steps to fill in order to do my present job adequately.

☐ Have my organizational rewards to date been equal to my organizational contributions and accomplishments? If not, why not?

☐ Have my attained career goals met my basic and underlying needs? For example, does my present job adequately meet my basic needs for power, recognition, status, mastering difficult problems, demonstrating my various competencies, having positive work relationships, providing time for all-round living? Alan Schoonmaker has prepared a detailed treatment of career goals compared to psychological needs for the manager interested in broad career analysis.

☐ Overpromotion: Honestly looking at my career achievement, am I now, or have I been in the past five or ten years, seriously overpromoted in terms of my ability to do the assigned job?

☐ Burnout: Have I been involved in serious psychological or physiological job stresses during the past five years that could lead to a burnout situation?

☐ Balanced living: Would I classify myself as a workaholic or a compulsive worker in developing my career to date? Have I been able to balance work and career interests with those related to family, to community, and to my own hobbies and interests?

Trying to be as objective as possible, rate yourself on your career achievements and satisfactions in Self-Analysis Chart 4.

**Self-Analysis Chart 4. Your career achievements
and satisfactions.**

ITEMS FOR EVALUATION	Definite plus + +	Somewhat plus +	Neutral 0	Somewhat minus −	Definite minus − −
1. Actual achievements compared to my hopes and expectations.	___	___	___	___	___
2. Progress up the career ladder in my field in terms of level attained.	___	___	___	___	___
3. Progress in terms of time and energy required to reach my present level.	___	___	___	___	___
4. Career skills—developed as I went along so that I am competent to handle a promotion.	___	___	___	___	___
5. Career skills—present job. Skills adequacies for present job.	___	___	___	___	___
6. Rewards-contribution: career rewards in relation to my organizational contribution.	___	___	___	___	___
7. Career goals—personal needs. My goals have related closely to my needs.	___	___	___	___	___
8. Overpromotion: not promoted too fast or too frequently for skills-capacities level?	___	___	___	___	___
9. Burnout: no significant physiological or psychological stresses now or at any earlier time?	___	___	___	___	___
10. Balanced living: career in balance with family, community and self-interests and commitments?	___	___	___	___	___

Self-Analysis Chart 4 continued.

	+ +	+	0	−	− −
11. Anticipated future career advancements: can I reasonably expect further advancements?	___	___	___	___	___
12. Career opportunities—planned career development: ability to make own opportunities through performance and selling myself.	___	___	___	___	___
13. Career opportunities—recognized: ability to see and take advantage of career opportunities as these develop through job assignments, special projects, committees, etc.	___	___	___	___	___
14. Career crises—survival: ability to weather the storm during cutbacks, layoffs, reorganizations, etc.	___	___	___	___	___
15. Career crises—anticipation: ability to anticipate possible future career crises that may arise during organizational changes, crises, etc., and to minimize their impact on my own career or else avoid them altogether.	___	___	___	___	___
Self-analysis subtotals	___	___	___	___	___

Looking at my career to date, I would say that, in balance, my two strongest career points are:

1. _____

2. _____

My two career points in greatest need of development are:

1. _____

2. _____

EVALUATING YOUR WORK RELATIONSHIPS

Since managers spend much of their working time either on the job or thinking about it, the nature of their working relationships, as these relationships do or do not meet the individual's emotional needs and interpersonal transactional expectations, have much to do with his total work-world satisfactions.

Because of the frequently fluctuating nature of work in complex organizations, work relationships among managers in such institutions have a good deal of built-in stress. For example, in a garment factory, if the department that cuts the garments turns out poor work, the sewing department, which has to put these pieces together, has difficulties. Particularly in the *long-linked technologies* where one department's finished products become the raw material with which the next department does its work, there exists the strong possibility of interpersonal and interdepartmental disagreements.

Organizational reward systems too often compound frictions initially generated by work flows. When peer-level managers compete for relatively few promotions at the next level up, hostilities and resentments are quite apt to surface. In such a win-lose situation, one manager gains his promotion at the expense of his peers. In addition, salary and pay plans are often set up on a functional basis. In such plans, there is little direct monetary incentive for peers to really pull together. It is in the *organizational interface areas*—the gray areas between functions or departments—that these frictions tend to build up.

If the tone and tenor of your work relationships have deteriorated markedly during the past two or so years, this may be a sign of increasing work friction. One effort to reduce interpersonal friction comes through the *profit center*. In a well-run profit center, managers realize that they have a common fate; that is, the group or profit-center bonus is so structured that one individual cannot win at the expense of his fellows.

Another approach to improving interpersonal relationships is a management-development program that qualifies each individual manager for promotion on a planned basis. Theoretically, this takes some of the advancement striving competitiveness out of peer-level relationships. Unfortunately, neither the profit-center concept nor most management-development programs eliminate peer conflicts completely.

Those organizations that operate on a crisis-management basis are most likely to have negative interpersonal relationships on the job. Crisis management (with its predilection to push, blame, and crash-program solutions to problems that are handled much more smoothly in the *professionally managed organization*) is a prime generator of interpersonal friction.

Self-Analysis Chart 5 is structured to help you to evaluate the *general tone and tenor* of your work relationships since the beginning of your managerial career.

Self-Analysis Chart 5. Your work relationships.

ITEMS FOR EVALUATION	Definite plus $++$	Somewhat plus $+$	Neutral 0	Somewhat minus $-$	Definite minus $--$
1. Relationships upward —with my present boss	___	___	___	___	___
2. Relationships upward —with my past bosses	___	___	___	___	___
3. Relationships upward —with people one or two levels above my boss	___	___	___	___	___
4. Lateral relationships with peers (considering job pressures and the normal competitive strivings)	___	___	___	___	___
5. Downward relationships—supervision—work output: how my subordinates and I relate in getting the unit's job done.	___	___	___	___	___

Self-Analysis Chart 5 continued.

	+ +	+	0	–	– –
6. Downward relationships—leadership: how my subordinates and I relate as a work team in getting the job done.	___	___	___	___	___
7. Ability to handle difficult work relationships:					
A. With superiors	___	___	___	___	___
B. With peers	___	___	___	___	___
C. With subordinates	___	___	___	___	___
8. Ability to handle crises and emergencies (without interpersonal relationships deteriorating unreasonably)					
9. Informal relations: social relationships at off-the-job parties, functions, etc., with people I work with.	___	___	___	___	___
10. Close interpersonal relationships: rewarding and mutually beneficial relationships with one or more of the people I work with.	___	___	___	___	___
Self-analysis subtotals	___	___	___	___	___

As I look at my present work relationships from the standpoint of a mid-career manager, I feel my two greatest strengths in this area are:

1. _____

2. _____

The two greatest areas for development in my present work relationships are:

1. _____

2. _____

YOU AND THE WORLD AROUND YOU

The problem of living intelligently in a confusing world is complicated. During each period of human history in which rapid or deep socio-technical changes take place, many individuals experience discomfort. Will Durant has written entertainingly about the great changes of history in his multivolume work. Peter Drucker, the management specialist, writes about today's changes. Dennis Gabor, Nobel Prize–winning physical scientist, suggests a new social model, while Herman Kahn and his associates give their idea of what life may be like in the relatively short run.

The satisfactions or dissatisfactions one gets from living in a society at a particular point in time are partly objective and partly subjective. Our society is reputed to have the highest general standard of living ever attained. Material goods abound. Most managers, in fact, struggle to keep track of all the *things* that are stored in their houses and garages. Yet there is also reported to be a general and pervasive individual dissatisfaction with our social, economic, and political world today.

As objectively as possible, please use Self-Analysis Chart 6 to evaluate the impact that the social and material world you live in today has on your feelings and satisfactions.

Self-Analysis Chart 6. Societal and other factors that affect you.

ITEMS FOR EVALUATION	Definite plus + +	Somewhat plus +	Neutral 0	Somewhat minus −	Definite minus − −
1. Social world: political and economic aspects of the world you live in	_____	_____	_____	_____	_____
2. Material world: house, cars, machines, conveniences, etc.	_____	_____	_____	_____	_____
3. Commuting situation: distance, time spent, difficulty of travel	_____	_____	_____	_____	_____
4. Living situation: city, neighborhood, house or apartment	_____	_____	_____	_____	_____
Self-analysis subtotals	_____	_____	_____	_____	_____

In reviewing my current mid-career situation in terms of society and things, I feel my two greatest strengths in this area are:

1. _____

2. _____

The two areas that would benefit from better understanding and/or situation improvement are:

1. _____

2. _____

EVALUATING YOUR OFF-THE-JOB SOCIAL RELATIONSHIPS

Because managers typically spend a great deal of energy in job and career activities, it is often difficult for them to develop close, positive, and supportive interpersonal ties with other individuals, particularly off the job. In addition, the manager's competitive career strivings and his tendencies to be a loner in the community he lives in because of the time demands of his job further impede his ability to develop deep social relationships that could be mutually stimulating and rewarding.

Yet mid-career is often a time when the individual would benefit from sharing and exchanging his or her deeper perceptions, concerns, and problems with a sympathetic "other." A friendly sounding board or an interested party with whom one could bounce ideas and feelings around is often an extremely valuable asset in assisting the mid-career manager in clarifying his perceptions, feelings, and decisions.

Extroverts usually have more personality and temperamental inclinations and skills with which to develop deeper friendships than do introverts. Yet interpersonal-competence skills are learnable by all. This type of skill improvement in mid-career will give the manager important additional resources with which to build positive and mutually beneficial social and work relationships.

How would you rate your present off-the-job social relations in terms of personal satisfactions and the extent to which they provide warm, positive, sharing exchanges of ideas, thoughts, and feelings? Self-Analysis Chart 7 should prove to be a helpful checklist.

Self-Analysis Chart 7. Your off-the-job social relationships.

RELATIONSHIPS WITH	Definite plus + +	Somewhat plus +	Neutral 0	Somewhat minus −	Definite minus − −
1. Close relatives: parents, grandparents, uncles, aunts, cousins	_____	_____	_____	_____	_____
2. In-laws	_____	_____	_____	_____	_____
3. Close friends: people with whom you have much in common or with whom you enjoy spending your time	_____	_____	_____	_____	_____
4. Social acquaintances: nonbusiness acquaintances made through hobbies, social contacts in your community, etc.	_____	_____	_____	_____	_____
5. Your spouse	_____	_____	_____	_____	_____
6. Your female children	_____	_____	_____	_____	_____
7. Your male children	_____	_____	_____	_____	_____
8. Any other social contacts	_____	_____	_____	_____	_____
Self-analysis subtotals	_____	_____	_____	_____	_____

As I view the social-relationships aspect of my life, the two strongest areas are:

1. _____

2. _____

The two areas in which I would benefit most through change and improvements are:

1. _____

2. _____

EVALUATING YOUR SOCIAL HISTORY

Self-analysis is a problem in the sense that it is hard for us to be completely objective about ourselves. Nevertheless, it can be a rewarding experience to the degree that it gives us insights into our basic life-style patterns. We can also gain insights by reviewing and evaluating our own social history. Self-Analysis Chart 8 lists the life-stage categories developed by Professor Levinson at Yale. Review each stage in terms of your own life and evaluate it as objectively as possible on the chart.

Self-Analysis Chart 8. Your social history.

LIFE STAGES (LEVINSON MODEL)	Definite plus + +	Somewhat plus +	Neutral 0	Somewhat minus —	Definite minus — —
1. Ages 16–22. Pulling up roots: establishing independence and ego identity.	_____	_____	_____	_____	_____
2. Ages 22–29. Provisional adulthood: getting established in career; forming intimate social relations.	_____	_____	_____	_____	_____
3. Ages 29–32. A transition period: review of your achievements vs. dreams and ambitions up to this point.	_____	_____	_____	_____	_____
4. Ages 32–39. Settling down: concentration on achievement via job, career, family and community routes.	_____	_____	_____	_____	_____
5. Ages 39–43. Potential mid-career crisis period: life review in mid-career; strong dissatisfactions with life to date may cause abrupt behavioral changes or feelings of resignation to one's fate.	_____	_____	_____	_____	_____

Self-Analysis Chart 8 continued.

	+ +	+	0	−	− −
6. Ages 43–50. Re-establishing and flowering period: coming to terms with one's life in a positive sense; mature creativity, productivity and life satisfaction.	____	____	____	____	____
Self-analysis subtotals	____	____	____	____	____

As I analyze my life history to date in terms of the Yale model, I feel that the two areas most beneficial to me were:

1. _____

2. _____

The two areas that may have left me with the greatest problems (that need work) are:

1. _____

2. _____

EVALUATING YOUR FLEXIBILITY AND BALANCE

Individuals who live in times of deep and rapid social and technical change can best make the required personal adjustments if they have both flexibility and balance. Flexibility refers to the ability to see the major changes that are taking place in the world. It also means making a comfortable adjustment to these changes without giving up that which you feel is valuable and good in your past. Very rigid people have difficulty adjusting to the times. On the other hand, people with a low sense of ego-identity have difficulty in really knowing "who they are." As a result, they often wander through life adopting the latest fads and fashions without any deep sense of self.

See Self-Analysis Chart 9 and rate your flexibility and balance in terms of behavior, philosophy, personality, and managerial style.

Self-Analysis Chart 9. Your flexibility and overall balance.

ITEMS FOR EVALUATION	Definite plus ++	Somewhat plus +	Neutral 0	Somewhat minus −	Definite minus − −
1. Flexibility: ability to adjust realistically to the new without giving up what is good in the old.	___	___	___	___	___
2. Doer-vs.-manager balance: ability to be a manager most of the time but a doer when required.	___	___	___	___	___
3. Thought-vs.-action balance: adequate planning and analysis combined with prompt and effective action.	___	___	___	___	___
4. Introvertive-vs.-extrovertive balance: effective balance between warm, friendly, outgoing relationships and somewhat withdrawn introvertive patterns.	___	___	___	___	___
5. Emotional expression balance: effective balance between freely expressing my feelings and acting the role of the aloof, unfeeling individual.	___	___	___	___	___
6. Leadership style balance: neither a dominator nor an abdicator; lead by motivating and challenging.	___	___	___	___	___
7. Followship balance: neither overly dependent on my boss nor rebelliously independent; in general, have good boss relations.	___	___	___	___	___

Self-Analysis Chart 9 continued.

	+ +	+	0	–	– –
8. Organizational balance: ability to accept key organizational rules and goals and still exercise strong individual achievement and initiative in getting organizational results.	____	____	____	____	____
9. Activity-passivity balance: neither frenetically active nor completely passive.	____	____	____	____	____
10. Tension-relaxation balance: operate in a balanced manner; neither compulsively tense nor too relaxed.	____	____	____	____	____
11. Work-play balance: in terms of my total time-energy situation, work and nonwork hobbies, activities, and interests are in good balance.	____	____	____	____	____
12. Optimism-pessimism balance: good balance between confidence regarding positive outcomes and practical awareness of possible negatives.	____	____	____	____	____
Self-analysis subtotals	____	____	____	____	____

In terms of personal flexibility and balance, I feel my two strongest points are:

1. _____

2. _____

The areas in which I would most profit by self-improvement and behavior change are:

1. _____

2. _____

SUMMARIZING YOUR MID-CAREER BALANCE SHEET

In putting together a summary of your Mid-Career Balance Sheet (Self-Analysis Charts 1–9), remember that *underlying patterns and percentages* will be more significant than absolute numbers. Because of the somewhat subjective and personal nature of any self-analysis process, more is likely to be learned from studying your overall trends and patterns than from a preoccupation with number totals.

In the Summary Balance Sheet, copy down the subtotals from each of the categories you checked in the Self-Analysis Charts.

Summary Balance Sheet (Self-Analysis Charts 1–9)

EVALUATED ITEMS	Definite plus $++$	Somewhat plus $+$	Neutral 0	Somewhat minus $-$	Definite minus $--$
Chart 1. Rewards and benefits of your job.	——	——	——	——	——
Chart 2. Your management capacities and skills.	——	——	——	——	——
Chart 3. Your effectiveness in the organization.	——	——	——	——	——
Chart 4. Your career achievements and satisfactions.	——	——	——	——	——
Chart 5. Your work relationships.	——	——	——	——	——
Chart 6. Societal and other factors that affect you.	——	——	——	——	——
Chart 7. Your off-the-job social relationships.	——	——	——	——	——
Chart 8. Your social history (Levinson model).	——	——	——	——	——
Chart 9. Your flexibility and overall balance.	——	——	——	——	——
Self-analysis totals	——	——	——	——	——

USING YOUR MID-CAREER BALANCE SHEET:
IMPLICATIONS AND INFERENCES

The reader can put the self-analysis sections of this chapter to work in a society that still has a high-mobility potential. Our society also has become increasingly tolerant and accepting of divergent life-styles. Therefore, the reader can think of his various options and alternatives for mid-career change on a broad scale.

Present Implications

What are the present implications of your balance sheet in terms of the percentages of items that have been checked?
- ☐ Definitely plus
- ☐ Somewhat plus
- ☐ Neutral—neither a plus nor a minus in my life
- ☐ Somewhat minus
- ☐ Definitely minus

If you find that you have a high percentage of plus items in each of the key areas, you can reasonably conclude that your current mid-career adjustments and satisfactions are favorable. You are getting a good deal out of life. You also fit reasonably well into your mid-career situation.

Should you find that a significantly high percentage of the items fall into the neutral category, then you may be somewhat like Irvin, who suffered from a case of the bureaucratic blahs.

Irvin is actually a very effective manager and has a rather good overall situation. However, he doesn't get any particular degree of personal satisfaction out of his accomplishments and competencies. Life for him has gone somewhat sour in the middle years. But it doesn't have to continue drifting in that direction. Through insight and self-directed change, there are many things that Irv can do to switch from neutral to the definitely plus category. In Chapter 10 we will discuss how to bring off this sort of switch.

In case you discover that a high percentage of your self-analysis Balance Sheet checks fall into the somewhat minus or the definitely minus category, you have pinpointed for yourself certain areas for self-directed change and self-development. Ned, who solved his *overpromotion* problem via the self-directed-change route, made this shift in an intelligent and practical way.

Developing Useful Historical Perspectives

If you can avoid the natural human tendency to rationalize and, in some cases, to project while doing your analysis, you may well find that this life-history review gives you a number of useful cues and suggestions. To organize such historical perspectives, you might ask yourself these kinds of questions:

☐ Did the type of family I was raised in significantly influence my past and present life-style in discernable ways?

☐ In reviewing my life history in terms of Professor Daniel Levinson's model, can I spot any particularly significant life events in any of the basic categories that have strongly influenced my present situation?

☐ Looking at my work-related Balance Sheet percentages, are there any special aspects I ought to work at changing? For example, do the job, organization, relationships, and career subsections of my Balance Sheet indicate certain key areas to be worked on?

☐ In terms of society, things, and people, how do I come out in terms of pluses, neutrals, and minuses? What are the implications of these patterns for mid-career change and development?

☐ Looking at my personal Balance Sheet totals, how do I rate myself in terms of flexibility and balance?

Thinking about Priorities and Payouts

Adult education and self-directed change in our contemporary society encourage the individual to use his own initiatives and competencies as much as possible in bringing about the desired new situation. Humanistic psychologists and transactional analytical psychologists both have placed a great deal of emphasis on what the individual can do (with appropriate help from others when needed) to change his own life situation.

Two of the mid-career managers discussed in Chapters 1 and 2 are examples of such self-directed change. Al, who decided on the basis of a management-seminar experience not to work over-time, was able to make a positive change through practical self-analysis. As he reviewed his life-style, he realized that his life had a serious work-play imbalance. Once he made his decision, he had to learn the professional management skills of personal-time management and delegation. For Al, changing his job-role be-havior and self-concept as a compulsive workaholic was the ini-tial aspect of change, but then he had to follow it up with skills development.

In the case of Frank, "Mr. Troubleshooter," the question "Why do you always have to take on the tough jobs?" got him to think about his life pattern. Through reflection and awareness of the effects of job stress on his physical condition, Frank made a firm decision to delegate more work to his three assistants. As soon as he decided to change this pattern and to take some of the pressures off himself, he let go of some tough assignments he had formerly thought only he could do. The assistants were much happier with the new job challenges, and Frank soon felt ten years younger.

Obviously both Al and Frank have to guard against falling back into their old job-role patterns. When a mid-career manager has spent 20 or more years getting himself grooved into a par-ticular organizational role pattern, there is a natural tendency for him to lapse back into it out of habit. Careful attention to personal time-management practices is the best way for each manager to insure that he does not relapse.

In addition, Al and Frank must continue to think about the Flexibility and Balance subsections of their Mid-Career Balance Sheets. Since both managers had an imbalance in the work-play aspects of their lives for many years, they should give serious thought to continuing self-directed change in this area.

Adults who seek mid-career growth and change should work on the basis of their own priorities and payouts. Like Al and Frank, they should begin self-directed change in terms of the one or two key areas that will have the greatest impact on their effectiveness and overall life satisfactions. Undoubtedly as each man reviews his personal Mid-Career Balance Sheet, he will find additional high-priority, high-payout areas that he can profitably work on in the years ahead.

However, if each manager *continues to work only on the particular areas he has selected,* he will find his mid-career satisfaction and effectiveness are appreciably improved. That is the reason for the emphasis on considering balance-sheet scores and percentages in terms of priorities and payouts.

If he begins with a single priority item where self-directed change will bring a high payout in terms of life satisfaction and career and personal growth, the rewards he receives from the new behavior will serve as reinforcements. They will also encourage him to continue along on his Action Plan for self-development in mid-career.

Behavior-modification psychologists point out the importance of reinforcement and of feedback on progress as each of us moves into our Action Plan for self-directed change. Chapter 10 will deal more specifically with the techniques for developing such an Action Plan.

SELECTED READINGS

For additional information on the skills of a professional manager, see Robert F. Pearse, "Certified Professional Management: Concept into Reality," *Personnel,* April–May, 1972.

Alan Schoonmaker, *Executive Career Strategies* (New York: AMACOM, 1969).

Will and Ariel Durant, *The Story of Civilization* (New York: Simon & Schuster, 10 volumes, 1935–1967).

Dennis Gabor, *The Mature Society* (New York: Praeger, 1972).

Herman Kahn and B. Bruce Briggs, *Things to Come* (New York: Macmillan, 1972).

10/Setting Up
an Action Plan
for Self-Development

WHEN THE manager thinks about self-directed change in mid-career, he necessarily thinks about where he has been in his earlier life; what the effects of some experiences have been on his present situation; where he sees himself now; where he can reasonably expect to go in the future; and the best way to get from here (the present) to there (the future).

SUCCESS AND THE SUCCESS ETHIC

Our society has placed a great deal of emphasis on individual success and achievement. Managers by and large find that a good deal of their personal motivations are intertwined with the American success ethic and notions about individual self-worth and successful achievement. But there are many indications that our national concept of success is changing. In a landmark study of what managers currently think about success and about the changing American success ethic, Dale Tarnowieski uncovered some important changes in the definition of success as managers view it:

> . . . An overwhelming 83 percent of the businessmen who responded to the questionnaire agree that attitudes towards success are changing. In fact, only respondents over sixty years of age seem to question this assertion to any significant degree. It is also interesting to note that virtually no difference in opinion exists between those respondents who say they are completely satisfied and those who say they are not satisfied with their personal and professional success.

> What is the nature of the change in success-related attitudes as survey respondents see it? Few businessmen believe that greater material reward is representative of success for most people. Nearly half of all respondents contend that success is increasingly measured in terms of job satisfaction and more meaningful work. What is especially noteworthy is the significant percentage of respondents (34%) who say that success increasingly represents the realization of goals and aspirations that may have little or nothing to do with career advancement.

SUCCESS AND TOTAL LIFE SATISFACTION

In setting up one's Action Plan, the manager ought to think first about what success and life satisfaction mean for him personally. This should be his starting point. Without such a base frame of reference, he has no fixed position from which to navigate his course in mid-career.

Since his career is often the basis from which he derives his life satisfactions, this book has placed considerable emphasis on work-related self-analysis. For some managers, career success in itself may be a large factor in their feelings of self-worth. Others may see their careers more as a means to an end. For them, work is a way to earn money, which in turn permits them to maintain a standard of living and subsidizes them in pursuit of nonwork activities.

Social considerations are also important to one's total life satisfaction. If an individual becomes too far removed from the mainstreams of the world he lives in, anomie, alienation, and dispiritation are likely to occur. Regardless of material success on the job, life for the alienated person holds little meaning and little satisfaction.

Personal factors are similarly important. Each of us has some degree of behavioral flexibility. We usually have a range of possible behavior that is larger than our habitual behavior. In some ways, self-directed change and personal growth in mid-career are devices by which we extend our habitual behavior closer to our range of possible behavior. If we try to go beyond our personal range of comfortable possible behavior, in the process of change we are likely to set up too great a degree of dissonance between what we are and what we attempt to become. This dissonance level may become so uncomfortable that we cannot support our new behavior without great internal strain.

BREAKING FREE OF CULTURAL CONDITIONING AND SELF-IMAGE

If self-directed change is to be successful for most of us, it must also include some device for stepping out of our usual ways of viewing ourselves and the world. Don Hamachek suggests a number of ways of doing this.

Once we have taken an objective look at our self-concept and self-images, we are in a better position to realistically assess the resources we possess for personal growth. Sometimes what holds us back most is an old negative or action-inhibiting way of viewing ourselves. Once these images are restructured in a more positive manner, the next thing to examine is ingrained habit patterns and habitual interpersonal transactional styles such as those discussed in the section on evaluating personal flexibility and balances in Chapter 9. By referring to this section, the manager can think constructively about his past and present tendencies and patterns in these two categories.

NEW PERSPECTIVES: THEIR IMPORTANCE TO THE CHANGE PROCESS

We will look at some mid-career manager cases from previous chapters to aid us in developing necessary perspectives for action planning. In most cases in which the manager made a successful change in mid-career, his ability to attain new or different perspectives was an important part of the process.

Once we have developed such perspectives, a further step is to consider realistic possible options and alternatives. Usually this is no great problem. For example, once Al, our chronically overtime-working manager, and Frank, Mr. Troubleshooter, each got a new perspective on his mid-career situation, many of the change options available to them soon became clear. For successful mid-career change and development, the individual then has to practice new behavior patterns or acquire new skills that will make him more successful in his mid-career situation.

APPLYING THE ACTION PLAN MODEL TO SELECTED CASES

Some of the vignettes given earlier are used here as general guides to assist the reader in setting up his own Action Plan model for self-directed change. Since people are inherently complex, some of the cases might logically apply to more than one problem area. To make these analyses operationally useful, we have to set up a sample model as a frame of reference. In each case we shall try to analyze the key problem or issue that seems to be the most significant in each manager's mid-career situation, and to consider key aspects of possible Action Plans that each manager might set up for himself. The Action Plan options suggested here offer a few of the practical solutions available to the manager.

Situation 1

Dave, a regional sales manager for a large organization, is caught in a win-lose competitive situation with the corporate product-manager group, which controls the purse-strings and calls the shots in terms of marketing strategy.

Key Factors. Dave could analyze his situation from a number of angles:

☐ Top corporate decision makers are currently enamored of the product-manager concept and feel this will solve many problems.

☐ The product managers feel superior, as a group, to the regional sales managers at Dave's level because of the difference in education. Most product managers have had little or no field sales experience and therefore are not familiar with what is going on in the field.

☐ The product managers are inclined to bury their judgmental errors. They blame the field sales force for "poor execution of a brilliantly conceived product-marketing plan" when things don't come out as envisioned.

Some Action Plan Options. At this point in his organizational career, Dave has a number of options:

☐ Wait until corporate management sees the weaknesses of their current product-marketing model.

☐ Use more persuasive communication in selling his ideas to product marketing. Even though the product-management group may get a portion of the organizational credit for Dave's recommendations, he gets the money to increase his region's sales.

☐ Take evening courses in M.B.A. areas that would give him more competence in product marketing. Dave might even get an evening M.B.A. degree. Once his product-management marketing skills are strengthened, Dave will be in a better position to influence the marketing managers.

Situation 2

Jim, formerly an outside consultant, was hired as an internal consultant by the corporation's president. The president sent Jim to Subsidiary X with the general instructions, "Improve profits as quickly as possible." In the process of playing an internal consulting role with his old external consulting slam-bang style, Jim alienated and made strong enemies of the subsidiary president and his two vice-presidents.

Key Factors

☐ An early group meeting with the corporate president, subsidiary president and his assistants, and Jim would have clarified Jim's specific assignment.

☐ Jim is currently caught in a classic win-lose competitive situation. If he can adapt his managerial style to a more conciliatory, joint-problem-solving posture, he has a better chance of winning the cooperation of the three key executives in the subsidiary company.

Some Action Plan Options

☐ Jim needs to realize that his old external consultant's style is inappropriate in his new assignment and to take a good hard look at the results he is likely to get in an internal consulting situation. If he wants to avoid this kind of win-lose situation in the future, he will have to change his interpersonal style on the job.

☐ It may be too late for Jim to bail himself out in the sense of winning the necessary cooperation of the people he works with. He may have to go to the president, lay the facts on the line, and perhaps get himself transferred to another assignment.

☐ Another choice is for Jim to get more professional managerial skills in bringing about planned change. His organization assignments put him in the role of an agent of change. Acquiring these skills might take time, money, and effort on Jim's part, but the long-range career payout would be in his ability to effect more lasting and deeper relationships and to be more effective on the job.

Situation 3

Art is the old-line plant manager in a metals company who literally fights with the young engineering and marketing type whom top management brought in to change the company's approach to doing business.

Key Factors

☐ Art's diagnosis was done for him by the young marketing-oriented engineer who was his peer in the management seminar. He bluntly told Art that if the latter were in his company, he would be fired, pushed aside, or given early retirement because of his negative behavior.

□ Art's company now wants more emphasis on special products and on customer technical service. Art's basic problem, viewed in this light, centers around how to adjust his managerial style and philosophy to the company's new way of doing business.

Some Action Plan Options

□ Art needs to realize that top corporate management is making a fundamental change in its marketing and production strategies. Until he develops adequate insight regarding the new situation and adjusts to it, his future career with the company is likely to be all downhill.

□ When he accepts the fact that a new day has dawned, Art's most probable high-payout Action Plan involves examining his past attitudes and behaviors in terms of what they are doing to him and to the company, and changing his managerial style—his perceptions, philosophy, and interpersonal transactions, particularly with the marketing-oriented engineers.

Situation 4

Over a five-year period, Charlie was continually promoted in the operations end of a very-fast-growth company. His warm, friendly, outgoing interpersonal style was not enough to enable him to manage effectively when he reached a top-level operating job. When the company brought in a very-well-qualified outsider, Charlie chose to resign.

Key Factors

□ A major part of Charlie's problem was the company's practice of overpromoting conscientious performers before they were qualified for the new job.

□ During the five-year period, Charlie received potentially useful feedback on some management areas in which he had limitations. Yet neither he nor the company set up a systematic program for his managerial development. Such a program would have given Charlie skill improvements that would have enabled him to handle his increased job responsibilities.

☐ Instead of working at his own skills development and hiring well-trained key subordinates, Charlie continued on with his formerly successful field-operations management pattern. However, this pattern became less successful as the company adopted new, more sophisticated management systems during its fast-growth phase.

Some Action Plan Options

☐ Charlie could have gotten additional psychological testing five years ago to give him a complete personal assessment. He then could have used this information as a basis for acquiring necessary skills in those areas in which he was weak.

☐ Also, he could have become more alert to the changes in the basic nature of his management job as he was promoted. As he moved closer to the top job in the organization, much more planning, measuring, and coordinating was required of him.

☐ He might have chosen to remain at a lower management level that he could handle, even if it were below the one he attained before leaving.

☐ His highest-payout Action Plan would have been to set up a personal training and skills upgrading program during the five-year period of his rapid advancement. Ned, another of our mid-career managers, did just that, successfully solving his own overpromotion problem through a planned self-improvement program.

Situation 5

Larry, a highly trained technical specialist, was hired by a fast-growth client company as a corporate specialist. Later he was moved into an administrative vice-president's job. This job expanded to twice its original size. His limited abilities, as a manager and supervisor, then put him under heavy physiological and psychological stress. After a physical problem developed, he was transferred back to his original job as a technical specialist. This was done not only for health reasons but because top management recognized his limitations as a key administrative vice-president.

Key Factors

☐ Neither Larry nor the company gave adequate consideration to his fundamental lack of skills in managerial leadership and supervision. The company hoped that he would somehow acquire necessary skills on the job. Unfortunately, Larry's managerial style was such that it was difficult for him to admit to others that he needed to learn anything new. As a consequence, he tried to muddle through and failed.

☐ Feedback from dissatisfied subordinates finally alerted top management to Larry's problems when these managers asked for transfers. But despite this, neither Larry nor top management set up a training program for him.

Some Action Plan Options

☐ He could have requested a chance to manage a smaller unit; or to begin with, he could have remained as a highly paid technical specialist on the top corporate staff and not have attempted to become a manager of a large administrative unit for which he was not qualified.

☐ Larry might have admitted that his growing psychological and physiological stresses were caused by his job. His career ambitions, which unfortunately were not matched by required skills, prevented him from being sufficiently objective to recognize that he could have taken steps such as courses in supervision, leadership, MBO, delegation, and motivating others to improve his skills and reduce his overall stress load.

Situation 6

After many years as a manufacturing engineer and plant manager in a large corporation, Paul was hired as a vice-president in charge of manufacturing by an entrepreneur-owner of a smaller company. At the same time, the entrepreneur hired a marketing vice-president from another large corporation. Paul and the marketing vice-president are currently locked in a win-lose struggle for power and possibly for organizational survival. Because of this feud, the company is losing both business and profits.

Key Factors

☐ Paul's own competitive strivings plus his combative nature cause him to approach this situation in an adversary relationship. So far, he has not considered the necessity for a new approach.

☐ The entrepreneur-owner is also at fault in not assisting Paul and his marketing peer to operate more on a team basis. The peer may be hostile and competitive in his relationships with Paul. The question is, can Paul improve this crucial situation by changing his own approach?

☐ Paul is throwing his weight around in this small company. He keeps reminding new associates that "this is the way we used to do it in Corporation X." Paul's patronizing approach does not win friends and influence people in his new company.

Some Action Plan Options

☐ Paul's probable best high-payout option is to get further training and skills development in interpersonal relationships and persuasive communication. His present hostile, competitive, win-lose style is not really helping anyone.

☐ Paul can also benefit by upgrading his skills as a general manager with a marketing- and finance-oriented outlook.

☐ Paul can become a more positive influence in the organization by being more concerned with overall organizational profits and growth and less concerned about outpointing his current rival. If the present win-lose situation continues, the entrepreneur-owner may have to fire both men and look for more cooperative key assistants.

Situation 7

Ted has worked in the corporate financial division of a very large firm for a number of years. Rotational overseas assignments are almost mandatory for higher career advancement in this organization. Ted lost out in his bid for a choice overseas assignment in France. He reluctantly took what he considered a second-best assignment in South America. Neither he nor his wife are happy in this assignment.

Key Factors

☐ One of Ted's key problems is his basic attitude of superiority and aloofness. People who aren't "his kind" get short shrift. The nationals in the country he is currently working in are almost bound to sense his feelings.

☐ Ted resented losing out on his bid for the better assignment. He lets this resentment show on his present job.

☐ He feels that in this overseas assignment he is operating beneath the level of his M.B.A.-degree training. He sees this job as also being beneath the staff level in which he was functioning at corporate headquarters. He is slightly aware that his attitudes of hostility, resentment, and superiority may be a factor in his being no more than an average performer on this assignment.

Some Action Plan Options

☐ Ted's greatest improvement area lies in his gaining more insight into the ways in which his present attitudes and managerial style affect his job performance and work relationships. There are a number of managerial self-awareness courses he can take that will expose him to techniques for improvement in these areas.

☐ He might leave this large corporation after this tour of duty and move to a smaller firm, where he might be accepted as the "expert" he longs to be.

☐ He can work more closely with the vice-president of the foreign subsidiary he is now with to gain a better general-management orientation in the international business field.

☐ He can stop playing the "ugly American" role on this overseas tour and get to know the country and people on a more positive and accepting basis. To begin with, he could develop an interest in the art, music, and cultural history of the country. If Ted and his wife have special hobbies or interests that would bring them into more positive contact with local nationals, they could build better relationships accordingly.

Situation 8

Ralph, a successful manager who came up the hard way with limited formal education, saw his son get married rather than go on to college. For Ralph as for other mid-life parents, part of the problem lies in the attitudinal gap between the generations. Ralph and his wife had both worked since their early adult years to build safety and security through conscientious effort. When they saw their son giving up the college opportunity they hadn't had, they were inclined to throw up their hands and say, "Let him go his own way; he won't listen to us."

The son, now 23, is divorced, living at home, and contemplating going to college again in pursuit of a career. Ralph's daughter is graduating from high school this year and is ready to start college.

Key Factors

☐ Ralph, like many mid-career managers who feel the generation gap between themselves and their children, is trying to interact with his children on a part parent, part fellow-adult basis.

☐ Any parent recently involved in a similar situation knows how difficult it is to work with one's grown children on an adult-to-adult joint problem-solving basis. In large part, this is because of the young person's own needs for independence and identity discovery. Listening in an objective way to what one's parents have to say is difficult for many young people in our society today.

☐ In many ways, Ralph has done his best. He maintained contact with his son through the marriage and divorce. He was admittedly biased against his daughter-in-law and, therefore, might not have done all he could to help the young couple make the marriage work. On the other hand, he is trying to be helpful without being parentally heavy-handed now that his son wants to begin his career. His daughter, by contrast, has no clear career interest, so he would like to see her attend a local community college until she has some idea of what she wants to do.

Some Action Plan Options. Because of the inherent complexities of intrafamily relationships, it is more difficult to develop an Action Plan in this area than in career-related areas. Even so, the mid-career manager can make significant improvements in his family life if he works intelligently at it. For example:

☐ Al, our mid-career manager who cured himself of compulsive workaholism and whose son refused to go college, maintained the relationship with his son on a reasonably positive basis. Eventually the son changed his perceptions and attitudes and decided to go to college.

☐ Ralph and his wife might take interpersonal-skills training such as that offered by Dr. Thomas Gordon, whose book seeks to help parents interact and communicate with their children on a joint problem-solving basis. When successful, it enables parents and children to interact much more effectively.

Situation 9

Bill is a very successful mid-career manager in a company that was recently merged with one of the giants in his industry. He is well-liked by the new owners and is considered to have a bright long-term career future as a staff specialist in his technical field. A college athlete who has just reached his early 40s, Bill resents the fact that he can no longer compete successfully in athletics with younger men.

Key Factors

☐ There may be many underlying facets to Bill's personal problem in which his self-image and self-concept seemingly cause him to resent the decline in his physical prowess.

☐ Evidently his concept of success and of life satisfaction is intimately linked with attitudes formed during his college years as a member of the university's varsity athletic team. He now feels uncomfortable when he goes back to fraternity reunions because most of the students there "look so young."

Some Action Plan Options

☐ Bill can keep himself in as good physical condition as possible and move his competitive athletic activities into the age-40-and-over category. This might not enable him to win over his 20-year-old son in athletic meets, but it might save Bill from possible serious physical problems.

☐ Bill might also dig a bit deeper into what from his early life experience causes him to put such great value on wining in athletic competition. In our youth-oriented society, he may simply be trying to hold onto his lost youth a bit longer than most. There might even be deeper underlying psychological reasons.

☐ Bill might go into part-time coaching in his favorite sport and pass his know-how on to the next generation. He could thus obtain vicarious gratification from helping younger people to become expert in his favorite sport.

☐ He can review his goals and priorities in terms of what "success" means to him personally now that he is a mid-career manager. If he must have an outlet for his competitive strivings, perhaps he can channel them into something physically less demanding.

Situation 10

Irvin's problem started out as one of bureaucratic blahs. Successful in a well-paying job as plant manager in a highly specialized industry, he has run his present plant well for several years. Essentially, he has little to complain about. However, the job holds little challenge and personal stimulation for him, and at this point, his job attitudes are beginning to affect his own self-concepts.

Key Factors

- ☐ Like many successful mid-career managers in well-paying jobs, Irvin can find little to complain about directly. In fact, his college classmates envy his success and his natural surroundings far from the pollution and congestion of big-city life.
- ☐ Lacking challenge and stimulation in his total life situation, Irv is obviously becoming depressed. Life is too predictable and routine; nothing interesting happens. He is not certain of his own achievements.
- ☐ Perhaps always on the introvertive side, he is beginning to withdraw into a shell. He is becoming less communicative. He tends to sit and stare out the window without doing anything for relatively long periods of time. The plant runs so smoothly, thanks to his leadership, that there is little for him to do on a daily operating basis.

Some Action Plan Options

- ☐ Irv can ask for a job transfer, either to another plant or to corporate headquarters. His track record indicates he is highly valued as a manager. The company unfortunately seems to have no adequate manager-development program.
- ☐ He can reschedule his business trips so as to bring more stimulation into his life. He and his wife, for example, could take an extra two or three days to stop over and visit interesting places when he has to go on a business junket.
- ☐ He can bring more challenge and stimulation into his life by getting more involved in community activities. Running for the school board, serving on the town council, and becoming involved in new arts and town social activities, for example, would give him more things to do.
- ☐ He can get more involved in his engineering professional society. He is liked and respected by his fellow professionals. He has only to get more involved in their association meetings and committee activities to introduce more stimulation into this aspect of his present life.

USING A THEORETICAL MODEL

Theoretical models are often useful for self-analysis. The accompanying diagram is a theoretical model illustrating how the elements of the Balance Sheet can be used to set up an Action Plan.

Building Your Mid-Life Action Plan Model

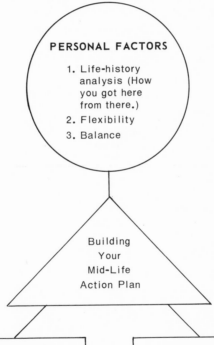

PERSONAL FACTORS

1. Life-history analysis (How you got here from there.)
2. Flexibility
3. Balance

Building Your Mid-Life Action Plan

WORK FACTORS

1. Job rewards and benefits.
2. Job capacities and skills.
3. Your effectiveness in the organization.
4. Career achievements and satisfactions.
5. Work relationships.

SOCIAL FACTORS

1. Society at large:
   -- the world we live in
   -- material possessions
   -- living and commuting
   -- impact of social and technological change
2. Social relationships
   -- community
   -- friends
   -- family and relatives

The reader can use the model to summarize his own thinking at this point.

SETTING REALISTIC ACTION PLAN GOALS

For the mid-career manager's efforts to bring maximum satisfaction, his change goals should be realistic ones that he can reasonably expect to reach with sources available to him and within a reasonable time frame. He will probably accomplish more if he works initially on the high-payout priorities that are most significant for him in relation to his personal concepts of "success" and "life satisfaction."

In the previous summaries, each mid-career manager had one or more key factors, areas that were most likely to give him useful handles for setting up his own Action Plan. Such a plan need not be extremely elaborate. Its beginnings could be as simple as Al's awareness that his chronic overtime pattern had a compulsive-workaholic aspect that he wanted to do away with. Once Al decided not to work overtime, he improved in the required managerial-skills areas through training.

Once Frank, Mr. Troubleshooter, developed a new perspective about his long-time organizational role, his action plan was simple: he just delegated more of these assignments to his able assistants.

It is true that both Al and Frank will have to be on the alert not to fall back into their old, deeply ingrained habits. They must also be careful not to get involved in equivalent activities (in the community or elsewhere) that essentially draw them back into the old patterns and pressures. If they can avoid these temptations, however, the rewards and life-satisfaction benefits that come out of their new life-style patterns should serve as adequate reinforcers to keep them on their new, more satisfying managerial paths.

Now, the time has come to analyze your Mid-Career Balance Sheet (developed in Chapter 9) and to look for the two or three areas where an effective Mid-Career Action Plan for self-directed change is most likely to have the highest chance of success (and

also is likely to bring you the greatest life-satisfaction payouts).
Please list those areas:

1. _____

2. _____

3. _____

    Now please list what you feel are the key underlying factors
in your present situation. Use as a guide the models and examples set up earlier in this chapter of brief mid-career case summaries plus relevent material from previous chapters.

1. _____

_____

2. _____

_____

3. _____

_____

4. _____

_____

5. _____

_____

SETTING UP YOUR SHORT-RANGE ACTION PLAN

Now that you have checked off the major areas for action planning from an analysis of your Mid-Career Balance Sheet and have analyzed what you believe to be the key underlying factors, you are in a position to set up a practical Action Plan for self-directed change. It might look something like this:

1. On the basis of my self-analysis, what realistic, practical steps can I take within the next 12 to 18 months to improve my mid-career situation?

A. _____

B. _____

C. _____

D. _____

2. Which of these steps can I reasonably expect to complete successfully through my own efforts and activities?

A. _____

B. _____

C. _____

D. _____

3. What will I need to successfully complete these steps on my own (in terms of such things as money, time, motivation, persever-

ance, skill acquisition, skill practice, self-concept change, work-situation analysis, and so forth)?

A. _____

B. _____

C. _____

4. What additional outside information or techniques might I need that I could get from reading books, taking courses, and the like?

A. _____

B. _____

C. _____

5. In which of the key areas might I have to turn to outside specialists for assistance (such as counseling, guidance, technical assistance in thinking through the problem situation, and so on)?

A. _____

B. _____

C. _____

6. How can I get usable feedback (in the sense of behavioral-modification reinforcement feedback) on progress toward my goals as I go through this self-directed change process?

A. _____

B. _____

C. _____

ACTION PLAN TIPS

The following subsections contain several suggestions that should prove helpful to you in setting up your Action Plan for self-directed change, and in insuring that your Plan yields successful results.

Where to Start

In each of the brief summaries analyzed in this chapter, there were a number of things that each mid-career manager could reasonably do on his own. Diagnosing the key aspects of one's present mid-career situation is usually the best place to begin. Because it is hard to be objective about ourselves unless we have had practice or training in this skill area, reading some of the books mentioned in various chapters will be a good starting point.

Use Specialists When Necessary

Successful self-directed change can often be best accomplished by getting the assistance of an outside specialist when you need it. For example, if Marvin, our mid-career manager who left one company partly because of his transactional patterns with the company president, finds that he tends to repeat these patterns in his new company, he may want to get outside assistance in diagnosing deeper, underlying aspects of these relationship patterns. Marvin may get adequate outside assistance through taking a course on self-awareness of managerial styles that his company pays for as part of its regular management-development program. Or he may need to get counseling or psychotherapy from a qualified practitioner if he feels that the problem requires additional outside assistance.

Tackle One Problem at a Time

One obstacle to successful change and growth in mid-career is the human tendency to do too many things too soon. Paul, our vice-president of manufacturing who is in a win-lose struggle with his marketing peer, for example, would benefit by simply changing his basic interpersonal approach.

If he does so and concentrates on communicating persuasively in terms of what is best for the organization (preferably through a simple but effective management-by-objectives program), there is every reason to believe that he can get out of his present locked-in competitive situation in a very positive manner. He may not have to do any deep self-analysis into his competitive strivings in order to make this behavioral change.

Make Easy Situational Changes Your Goals

It would be unreasonable to say that all mid-career problems can be solved through relatively simple changes in the manager's immediate work situation. Life isn't that easy for any of us. On the other hand, in this book we have looked at several case summaries of real-life managers. Many of them can make significant and substantial improvements in their circumstances if motivated. They have the intelligence and the action capacity to do many of these things on their own.

In some cases, a manager may require outside assistance to make the necessary transitions. If so, he shouldn't hesitate to get it. Moneywise, he can consider it a worthwhile investment. Such outside help will accelerate his self-directed change process to a significant degree.

Be Prepared to Invest Time and Energy

While some of the key aspects of Paul's change situation are not particularly difficult, they will require an investment of time, thought, and persistent attention to his old transactional patterns if he wants to change enough to build a new, permanent approach to work relationships.

THE ONGOING PROCESS OF SELF-DIRECTED CHANGE

Improving skills is, for most of us in managerial life, an ongoing process throughout our careers. As we advance in responsibility levels, we usually have to acquire new skills to handle the more difficult problems. The professional manager, then, is one who never has it completely made. He should always be seeking to improve his own effectiveness through increasing his managerial skills and capabilities. Becoming a professional manager and remaining one requires a lifetime commitment to developing, refining, and polishing one's managerial skills. Successfully solving the problems he encounters is only one aspect, albeit a very important one, of being a fully qualified professional manager.

Not all of the managers whose situations we have looked at in these case summaries have as yet solved their key mid-career problems. Perhaps some of them never will. Yet all of them, like all the readers of this book, are capable of improving their particular situation through intelligent self-analysis, self-understanding and *self-directed change*. Such change can and will lead them toward the attainment of the realistic self-development goals they set for themselves.

SELECTED READINGS

Dale Tarnowieski, *The Changing Success Ethic* (New York: AMA Survey Report, 1973).

Don E. Hamachek, *Encounters with the Self* (New York: Holt, Rinehart & Winston, 1971).

Thomas Gordon, *Parent Effectiveness Training* (New York: Wyden, 1970).

Michael Mahoney, *Self-Control: Power to the Person* (Belmont, Calif.: Brooks/Cole, 1972).

A. Robert Sherman, *Behavior Modification: Theory and Practice* (Belmont, Calif.: Brooks/Cole, 1973).

David L. Watson, *Self-Modification for Personal Adjustment* (Belmont, Calif.: Brooks/Cole, 1973).

Index